NUTS!

The Battle of the Bulge

By the Same Authors

The Way It Was: Pearl Harbor—The Original Photographs (1991)

D-Day Normandy: The Story and Photographs (1994)

By Donald M. Goldstein and Katherine V. Dillon

The Williwaw War (1992)

With Gordon W. Prange

(ed.) *The Pearl Harbor Papers: Inside the Japanese Plans* (1993)

At Dawn We Slept: The Untold Story of Pearl Harbor (1981)

Miracle at Midway (1982)

Target Tokyo: The Story of the Sorge Spy Ring (1984)

December 7, 1941: The Day the Japanese Attacked Pearl Harbor (1988)

Fading Victory: The Diary of Admiral Matome Ugaki (1991)

With Masataka Chihaya

God's Samurai: Lead Pilot at Pearl Harbor (1990)

By J. Michael Wenger and Robert J. Cressman

Infamous Day: Marines at Pearl Harbor, 7 December 1941 (1992)

Steady Nerves and Stout Hearts: The Enterprise (CV-6) Air Group and Pearl Harbor, 7 December 1941 (1989)

NUTS!

The Battle of the Bulge

The Story and Photographs

DONALD M. GOLDSTEIN, KATHERINE V. DILLON,

and J. MICHAEL WENGER

BRASSEY'S

WASHINGTON

Maps in figures 3-1, 3-33, and 6-10 by Thomas W. Dworschak.
Reproduced by permission of the AUSA Institute of Land Warfare
from "Hitler's 'Watch on the Rhine': The Battle of the Bulge,"
Land Warfare Papers, no. 12, September 1992. Maps in figures
4–1 and 5–18 by Derrick Chamlee/D.C. Design.

Library of Congress Cataloging-in-Publication Data

Goldstein, Donald M.
    Nuts! The Battle of the Bulge: the story and photographs/
Donald M. Goldstein, Katherine V. Dillon, and J. Michael Wenger.
        p.   cm.
    Includes index.
    Hardcover ISBN 0–02–881069–4   Paperback ISBN 1-57488-279-1
    1. Ardennes, Battle of the, 1944–1945.   2. Ardennes, Battle of
the, 1944–1945—Pictorial works.   I. Dillon, Katherine V.
II. Wenger, J. Michael.   III. Title.
D756.5.A7G65   1994
940.54′21431—dc20   94–9805
                                                         CIP

Designed by Robert Freese

10 9 8 7 6 5

Printed in Canada

Acknowledgments

This book would not have been possible without the cooperation of the many who graciously shared with us their expertise and interest. We especially wish to acknowledge the following who furnished ideas, materials, and information: Patterson Anthony, Richard Barnes, John D. Conner, Robert Cressman, Michael Grzebien, Martin Konopka, John Lambeth, John Lundstrom, Dr. Edward Schatz, and James J. Weingartner. Mark R. Wenger assisted in last-minute research in the National Archives. At that institution, Dale Connelly and Sharon Culley assisted in photo research, while Holly Reed handled our photograph orders. Others who assisted in photo research include Melissa Keiser of the National Air and Space Museum and Michael Winey of the U.S. Army Military Historical Institute. Gibson Bell Smith at the Suitland Records Center located the records of the massacre at Malmédy and Frau Edith Peffer fulfilled our requests for photographs and documents at the Bundesarchiv, while Celia Pratt of the University of North Carolina's Map Collection handled our requests for European maps.

We are deeply indebted to M. Jean Paul Pallud of Grenoble, France, the indefatigable "Bulge" historian par excellence. Without his scholarship, his tireless efforts tramping the highways and byways of the Ardennes, and his personal generosity to Wenger, the proper interpretation of the German photography contained in this work would not have been possible.

We also wish to acknowledge our debt to Jennifer Bosworth, Nathan Herman, Kendall Stanley, and Anita Tilford, and to Don McKeon and Carsten Fries of Brassey's for their technical service.

DONALD M. GOLDSTEIN, PH.D.
Professor of Public and International Affairs
University of Pittsburgh
Pittsburgh, PA

KATHERINE V. DILLON
CWO, USAF (Ret.)
Arlington, VA

J. MICHAEL WENGER, M.A.
Raleigh, NC

 **An AUSA Book**

The Association of the United States Army, or AUSA, was founded in 1950 as a not-for-profit organization dedicated to education concerning the role of the U.S. Army, to providing material for military professional development, and to the promotion of proper recognition and appreciation of the profession of arms. Its constituencies include those who serve in the Army today, including Army National Guard, Army Reserve, and Army civilians, and the retirees and veterans who have served in the past, and all their families. A large number of public-minded citizens and business leaders are also an important constituency. The Association seeks to educate the public, elected and appointed officials, and leaders of the defense industry on crucial issues involving the adequacy of our national defense, particularly those issues affecting land warfare.

In 1988 the AUSA established within its existing organization a new entity known as the Institute of Land Warfare. Its purpose is to extend the educational work of the AUSA by sponsoring scholarly publications, to include books, monographs, and essays on key defense issues, as well as workshops and symposia. Among the volumes chosen for designation as "An AUSA Institute of Land Warfare Book" are both new texts and reprints of titles of enduring value that are no longer in print. Topics include history, policy issues, strategy, and tactics. Publication as an AUSA Book does not indicate that the Association of the United States Army and the publisher agree with everything in the book, but does suggest that the AUSA and the publisher believe this book will stimulate the thinking of AUSA members and others concerned about important issues.

Contents

Preface

When one thinks of great battles, one visualizes large armies deploying against one another in well-planned patterns. The Battle of the Bulge did not fit that design. It was not a tapestry but a patchwork quilt—a multitude of small engagements played out in or near small towns, most of no military significance. Only when the individual patches are put together does the pattern become clear.

The many photographs taken in connection with the Ardennes Offensive contain little of the actual fighting, which is not too surprising. Even the most dedicated military photographer in the midst of battle would have had something on his mind other than snapping pictures. The photographs herein comprise the best available to give the reader an idea of the people, the weapons, and the movement of troops in the campaign and its distressing aftermath.

The book follows roughly a pattern the authors have used before and found effective. It is divided into nine chapters: Chapter 1, "The Antagonists," provides concise comments about the top U.S. and German commanders; Chapter 2, "Men and Machines," describes the opposing organizations and the weapons and vehicles upon which their men depended; Chapter 3, "The Battle Plan, Objectives, and Orders of Battle," outlines Hitler's plan for the Ardennes Offensive and the major units that would carry it out; Chapter 4, "The German Offensive Opens," depicts the German invasion routes, with most of the photographs reproduced from German films; Chapter 5, "German Special Operations, Massacre at Baugnez, Americans React to the Offensive"—the lengthy title is self-explanatory—features many photographs pertaining to the killings at Baugnez, better known as the Malmédy massacre; Chapter 6, "Bastogne Besieged," covers the best-known action of the Battle of the Bulge, or the siege of Bastogne; Chapter 7, "The German Offensive Slows," marks the turn of the tide; Chapter 8, "The Allies Crush the Bulge," recounts the Allies' final victory; and Chapter 9, "Aftermath," tells of the postwar investigation of the Malmédy massacre.

The student of World War II will recognize some of these photographs, but many are heretofore unpublished. Moreover, the photographs in Chapter 4 are shown here for the first time in proper order. Much of the material pertaining to the Malmédy massacre will also be unfamiliar.

We have used German ranks for authenticity and because no U.S. equivalent exists in many cases. We also have used German unit designations.

We have included no formal bibliography, but we list below a number of books dealing with the Ardennes Offensive that we believe are excellent and instructive. The following well deserve the attention of the reader who wishes to learn about this battle in detail: James Lea Cate and Wesley Frank Craven, *The Army Air Forces in World War II, Vol 3*; Hugh M. Cole, *U.S. Army in World War II: The Ardennes, Battle of the Bulge*; Danny S. Parker, *Battle of the Bulge: Hitler's Ardennes Offensive, 1944–45*; John S. D. Eisenhower, *The Bitter Woods*; Charles B. McDonald, *A Time for Trumpets*; James J. Weingartner, *Crossroads of Death: The Story of the Malmédy Massacre and Trial*; Jean Paul Pallud, *Battle of the Bulge: Then and Now*; Hermann Jung, *Die Ardennen-Offensive: 1944–45*; Samuel W. Mitcham Jr., *Hitler's Legions: The German Army Order of Battle, World War II*; and Georg Tessin, *Verbände und Truppen der Deutschen Wehrmacht und Waffen-SS im Zweiten Weltkreig: 1939–1945*.

The Battle of the Bulge was Germany's last desperate gamble and, for several weeks, held up the Allied advance. But in the end, Allied power prevailed, and Hitler had expended much of his country's final strength uselessly and hastened Germany's inevitable defeat.

We would like to dedicate this book to the men on both sides who fought bravely for the cause in which they believed.

Introduction

For approximately a month after the D-Day landings on 6 June 1944, the Allies' progress inland moved at a snail's pace. But once the Allies broke the impasse and left Normandy behind, their campaign moved rapidly and was soon ahead of schedule. The Allies' liberation of Paris on 25 August might have had no real military significance, but it had an enormous psychological impact. The City of Light, whose occupation had been the very symbol of Germany's domination of continental Europe, was free and in French hands again.

By the end of August, both Gen. Dwight D. (Ike) Eisenhower and his G-2 (intelligence officer), British Maj. Gen. Kenneth W. D. Strong, knew the end of the war was in sight. By October, the Combined Chiefs of Staff was exhorting Ike to end the war by the end of the year and, if necessary, to throw in every man and all matériel—forget about reserves. Eisenhower knew this goal was unrealistic, but he hoped that the Allies would possibly take the Ruhr River by 31 December.

One man who resisted the tide of optimism was Col. Oscar W. Koch, G-2 of Gen. George S. Patton's Third Army. He pointed out that, while the Germans were pulling back, their retreat was not a rout. Undoubtedly they would put up "a last-ditch struggle," and soon the winter weather and terrain would favor the Germans.

On the eve of the Ardennes Offensive, Eisenhower's forces ranged over five hundred miles from the North Sea to Switzerland. His major strength lay in the north, aimed for the Ruhr, while the balance was south of the Ardennes for the projected campaign toward the Saar River. This division of forces meant that the rest of the front would be defended very thinly.

The British forces were in the far northern point of the line, mainly in the Netherlands. In the southern-most portion of the front, mostly in Alsace, was the 6th Army Group, which included the U.S. Seventh Army and French First Army. North of the Ardennes was the 12th Army Group under Gen. Omar N. Bradley, whose Ninth

Army was north of Aachen. Lt. Gen. Courtney Hodges and his First Army were somewhat south of the city, with the Ardennes being one of Hodges's responsibilities. Patton's Third Army was in Lorraine.

Exactly why the Germans' Ardennes Offensive caught the Allies so flat-footed has never been adequately explained and possibly never will be. Although the Allies' Ultra machine busily translated messages from the Germans' Enigma machines, they picked up no direct hints, thanks to Adolf Hitler's order that nothing about the proposed plan be sent by wireless. However, the Allies did have other good intelligence sources. The photo-reconnaissance units of Lt. Gen. Hoyt S. Vandenburg's command, for example, netted more than enough intelligence for the Allies to have deduced the Germans' intentions during early December 1944. Despite atrocious weather, tactical reconnaissance units flew hundreds of sorties, reporting heavy rail activity both east and west of the Rhine River and detecting flat cars crammed with trucks, ambulances, and tanks. Marshaling yards were crowded, and increasingly this activity was happening west of the Rhine. One sortie discovered a convoy of twenty to thirty trucks bearing U.S. markings. Hospital trains were often seen west of the Rhine. They also spotted piles of what appeared to be supplies and stacks of lumber, with the latter suspected of being destined to build or repair bridges. On 14 December, a column of infantry was reportedly on the move near Monschau. The next day, over 120 vehicles were seen moving south from Heimbach. And much, much more.

None of this information seems to have aroused the interest one might expect. In fact, in a briefing the very day before the Germans struck, Ike's G-3 (operations and training officer) told some officers that there was nothing to report in the Ardennes sector. The Americans' failure to act in the face of these intelligence reports pointed to a Pearl Harbor–like failure. Possibly the army's intelligence-gathering infrastructure and the high command failed to communicate adequately with each other. And perhaps the patronizing attitude of the operations types toward the intelligence officers had something to do with this. The G-2 did not enjoy the degree of prestige accorded to the other "Gs." Thus, when intelligence conflicted with preconceived operational notions, all too often operations overlooked or explained away the facts.

One of those notions that seems to have been fairly widespread was that the Ardennes was a rather quiet sector. It was seen as a good location to send battle-weary troops for recuperation and to spot green units so that they might acquire a little field experience without running into real danger.

Of course, the U.S. top brass realized that the Allies' defense in the Ardennes was exceedingly thin, but they could not defend every place in equal depth. They took the calculated risk. Besides, the ever-practical Bradley pointed out, an attack had to have one of two objectives—to destroy enemy forces or to attain "a terrain objective"—and neither was attainable in the Ardennes.

In theory, Bradley was quite right, but he and others overlooked the fact that twice within the last thirty years—in World War I and again in 1940—the Germans had blitzed through the Ardennes for neither of Bradley's reasons. They had used the area instead as a highway toward their real objectives. Moreover, the Germans were now taking orders from a man whose mind was singularly ill-attuned to purely logical concepts.

Quite incapable of facing the prospect of real and final defeat, at this time Hitler clung to a few shreds of optimism. In the east, both Finland and Romania were out of the war, a condition mitigated by German's countermeasures in the south and by its withdrawal into Norway. Army Group (*Heeresgruppe*) North was cut off in Courland, extenuated once again by the fact that the Germans there tied down Soviet forces that might have been better deployed elsewhere. Farther south, following the collapse of Army Group Center, the Germans had been able to stabilize the front. Elsewhere, the *Wehrmacht,* although in retreat in the southeast sector of the Russian Front, was effecting an orderly withdrawal.

The embarrassing collapse of the German Army in France had come to a merciful end. Now, the Anglo-American offensive had slowed, due to increasing logistical and supply problems and to the prospect of encountering the last physical barriers blocking entrance to the German homeland—the Siegfried Line, as the Allies called the West Wall, and the Rhine River. In Italy, too, the front seemed to have stabilized. To combat the effects of the Allied bomber offensive that continued to lay waste to Germany's population centers and industrial cities, war production was decentralized and in some places even put underground so that production continued at full tilt in many areas.

Therefore, as 1944 drew to a close, Hitler felt that the *Wehrmacht* had regained some measure of control over the war, at least for the time being. Meanwhile, he reasoned, the Allies were overconfident and perhaps overextended. What better time for a surprise offensive on the Western Front? Despite the enormous risks involved, Hitler rightly concluded that the war could not be won by staying on the defensive. Germany now had one last Clausewitzian opportunity to seize the moment and to break up what he felt to be a fragile alliance.

Unfortunately for the Germans, at this point the Führer was most spectacularly unsuited to masterminding a project of this scope and complexity. His leadership style and personality traits had already begun to work a most destructive influence on Germany's prosecution of the war. Hitler had become obsessed with paper figures and quantities, oblivious to the fact that tanks and artillery shells produced in a factory did not necessarily mean that they were available to the front. Moreover, while Hitler had some grasp of how a division operated in the field, he had little concept of how an army functioned and a scant understanding of the staggering logistical considerations involved in maintaining his armies. Coupled with Hitler's failing mental faculties and his increasing inflexibility, this shallowness promised difficult days ahead for the *Wehrmacht.*

Finally, while the actual wounds he had suffered in the attempt on his life in the summer of 1944 were superficial, his health had deteriorated markedly since that incident. Always suspicious and vindictive, he was now paranoid of the very men on whom he had to rely to carry out his plans—his generals.

Could the Germans have won the Battle of the Bulge? Not in the long run, but they possibly could have prolonged it and thus delayed the ultimate Allied victory. Mulling over the "ifs" of history is fruitless but always fascinating. *If* Hitler had entrusted his major thrust to the 5. Panzer-Armee under the capable General der Panzertruppen Hasso von Manteuffel, the all-important early moves might have been swifter and more decisive. Instead, Hitler gave pride of place to the 6. Panzer-Armee, whose leader, Josef ("Sepp") Dietrich, was one of Hitler's old cronies and much less gifted than Manteuffel. *If* the offensive had reached the Meuse River, it might have swung northward as planned and trapped the U.S. forces near Aachen. *If* the Germans had captured Liège, they would have taken a massive Allied supply depot that could have prolonged their operations.

Of course, the farther Hitler's troops proceeded westward, the more units they would have had to transfer from the Eastern Front. This opens up the most intriguing possibility of all. Would the ever-opportunistic Soviet Union have held up its winter advance if Germany and the Allies were thus engaged in battle far away? Would Stalin have abided by any boundary agreements if he had seen the chance to reach not only Berlin but well beyond, perhaps to the Rhine?

Although none of this happened, the reality was bad enough. U.S. casualties in round numbers were 81,000, including 19,000 killed; 1,400 British casualties included around 200 killed. It is estimated that the Germans lost about 100,000 killed, wounded, and captured.

As with all battles, the Ardennes Offensive offered certain lessons for anyone disposed to learn them. As mentioned, twice before Germany had attacked through the Ardennes, hence any intimation of unusual German activity opposite the Ardennes should have received prompt and serious consideration.

At the time, Allied strategy was understandably focused on the offensive. But the possibility of a German strike always existed. An enemy is always dangerous, even in retreat and perhaps especially in retreat. Such an enemy, backed to the point where he is defending home borders, has everything to lose and may turn like a cornered animal.

In such a situation as the Allies faced in late 1944, the first line of defense should have been current intelligence and the facts based upon actual observation—not estimates of enemy intentions, not calculated risks, not preconceived ideas. If the Battle of the Bulge taught no other lesson than facts should outrank plans and theories, it would be well worth remembering this battle of long ago.

NUTS!

The Battle of the Bulge

CHAPTER 1

The Antagonists

THE AMERICAN LEADERS

In the early stages of every war, a certain number of unexpected and at times disconcerting adjustments occur in the officer corps. Men who have racked up years of impeccable peacetime service prove unable to function under the stresses of war, while others with acceptable but colorless records prove under fire to be the stuff of which leaders are made. By late autumn 1944, however, most such anomalies had been resolved. Those men in charge were known quantities who had been tested and had rung true.

In command of the First Army was Lt. Gen. Courtney H. Hodges (1–1). A modest man, he never courted publicity and might have ended his career in relative obscurity had not the Ardennes Offensive thrust him to the center stage. He entered West Point in 1904 but left before the end of his plebe year when he failed geometry. Not reconciled to losing his military career, he enlisted in the Infantry and won his gold bar only a year later than his former classmates.

Hodges went to Mexico with Gen. John J. Pershing's expedition in pursuit of Pancho Villa, and during World War I, he served in France with the 6th Infantry Regiment of the 5th Infantry Division. There, during the Meuse-Argonne campaign, he headed a machine-gun company, winning the Distinguished Service Cross and a promotion to lieutenant colonel. With the armistice, his rank reverted to major, and, as so many officers, he entered upon a long period of classroom duty. As either a student or an instructor, Hodges attended the Field Artillery School, Command and General Staff School, and the Air Corps Tactical School. Even West Point summoned back as a tactical officer the man it had cut from the corps.

His later assignments included serving with the Infantry Board, with the General Staff of the Philippine Department, and as the commandant of the Infantry School at Fort Benning, Georgia. By 1941 Hodges was chief of infantry, and, with World War II in full swing, in February 1943, he was promoted to lieutenant general with command of the Third Army. Sixteen months later, he landed at Normandy as deputy to Lt. Gen. Omar N. Bradley, whom he succeeded in command of the First Army.

1–1. Lt. Gen. Courtney H. Hodges, First Army (*left*). His command would bear the initial brunt of the German offensive. He is shown here with Maj. Gen. Maurice Rose of the 3d Armored Division in the Rhine Valley on 24 March 1945.

Hodges's self-effacing character has helped obscure the fact that his First Army moved farther and for the most part with more armor than the Third Army under the flamboyant Gen. George S. Patton. Fittingly, Hodges became known as the solider's soldier. The only senior American commander in the European theater to have served as an enlisted man at company level in combat, Hodges was enormously proud of and concerned with his men. As his First Army moved forward, he ensured that certain towns to the rear were designated as rest centers, where his combat troops could take it easy "within the limits of propriety."

The West Point class of 1915 would later be known as "the class the stars fell on." One of its members was Omar Bradley, the son of a Missouri schoolteacher (1–2). As so many of his contemporaries, he saw no combat during World War I. His service during the interwar years was unspectacular but solid. He drew the usual routine and teaching assignments, ultimately becoming commandant of the Infantry School. There he first met Chief of Staff George C. Marshall, who had an ability to spot real talent and recognized that in Bradley he had struck gold.

With the opening of World War II, Bradley's teaching assignments were over. He commanded the 82d Division prior to its conversion to airborne status and the 28th Infantry. In North Africa, Bradley served as the deputy commander of Patton's II Corps, later leading the corps in Tunisia and Sicily. Bradley and Patton were about as different in temperament and disposition as any two men could be, but each recognized the other's qualities and

they got along well. They continued to do so even later, when their positions were reversed and Patton served under Bradley.

After overseeing the landings at Normandy as commander of the First Army, Bradley took over the 12th Army Group later in 1944. Tactful, unselfish, and sincerely concerned for the men in his command, Bradley was one of the solid rocks in his classmate Eisenhower's command structure, which comprised a wide variety of talents and mentalities.

So much has already been written about Gen. Dwight D. Eisenhower (1–2), but we should stress that his role as commander of the Allied Expeditionary Force was as much a political burden as a military one. His usual demeanor of dignified amiability, his fatherly image, and the radiant smile that could melt an icicle at twenty paces made him an easy man to underestimate; but he could be pushed just so far. When his temper exploded, the fallout could be awesome. On one notable occasion, he reduced his old friend Patton to tears.

Perhaps even more than his compatriots, the Germans realized Ike's invaluable contribution to the Allied cause. Early in 1944, a lecture at the *Luftwaffe* Academy praised his energy, his ability to inspire his subordinates, and his diplomatic ability in bringing consensus to the diverse elements of the Grand Alliance.

Maj. Gen. Leonard T. Gerow (1–2) was not a West Pointer. Like Marshall, he was an honor graduate of Virginia Military Institute. He attended the Command and General Staff College with Eisenhower. Both graduated

1–2. (*Left to right*) **Lt. Gen. Omar N. Bradley, 12th Army Group; Maj. Gen. Leonard T. Gerow, V Corps; General Dwight D. Eisenhower, supreme commander, Allied Expeditionary Force; and Maj. Gen. J. Lawton Collins, VII Corps, in France on 21 July 1944.**

with honors, with Ike a fraction of a point ahead of "Gee," as Gerow's friends called him.

He had a preview of things to come when he was on duty in the Philippines with the 31st Infantry Regiment. He witnessed the fighting in Shanghai during the Japanese invasion of China. Gerow's stint as chief of the War Plans Division in Washington in the years just prior to World War II very nearly made him a political casualty of Pearl Harbor. However, his soldierly acceptance of a portion of the blame for that disaster was in pleasing contrast to the general testimony of alibis and blame, and he bounced back. In 1942, he took command of the 29th Infantry Division and then stepped up quickly to command the V Corps, a post he held through the Normandy campaign and the Ardennes Offensive. Gerow seemed to have a genius for putting his V Corps wherever the action was— Omaha Beach, the liberation of Paris, the Ardennes. A careful man of sound logic, Gerow won his third star as commander of the Fifteenth Army.

Maj. Gen. J. Lawton Collins (1–2) graduated from West Point in 1917 and was not sent overseas until after the armistice, when he participated in the occupation of Germany. His later duties included teaching at West Point and attending the General Staff and War colleges.

After Pearl Harbor, Collins went to Hawaii to organize the islands' defenses, and he remained in the Pacific, commanding the 25th Infantry Division at Guadalcanal. This division had been nicknamed "Tropic Lightning," and someone decided that Collins's initials J. L. stood for "Joe Lightning." Taking command of the VII Corps for the campaign in Normandy, Collins conducted the Cherbourg operation with such celerity that his nickname was reversed to "Lightning Joe" for the rest of the war. Both Hodges and British Field Marshal Bernard L. Montgomery thought highly of Collins.

Maj. Gen. Matthew B. Ridgway (1–3) was an army brat and knew no other life than the U.S. Army. Like his West Point classmate Collins, Ridgway did not receive a combat assignment in World War I, he was posted near the U.S.-Mexican border instead. Soon, however, his fluency in Spanish brought him to West Point as an instructor in that language. This talent may help account for his assignments to such Spanish-speaking countries as Bolivia, Nicaragua, and Panama. He also served in China, the Philippines, and stateside on various commissions and staffs and in the War Plans Division.

In March 1942, he became Bradley's deputy in the 82d Division and took command of that division during its transition to airborne status. He stayed with the 82d Airborne through all of its campaigns in North Africa, Sicily, and Normandy. In August 1944, he rose to command the XVIII Airborne Corps.

Ridgway was a hard taskmaster, but he was just as tough on himself; and his men admired him for this trait. He also had a habit of wearing a grenade taped to his chest

1–3. Maj. Gen. Matthew B. Ridgway (*left*), XVIII Airborne Corps, talks with the staff of the 82d Airborne Division near Ribera, Sicily, in late July 1943.

harness, not out of machismo, he explained; he simply thought he might need it.

Lt. Gen. George S. Patton Jr. (1–4) was a controversial figure whose unabashed ego stood in sharp contrast to the workmanlike professionalism of such men as Eisenhower and Bradley. Patton was just as dedicated as they were— this complex personality was first and foremost a professional soldier—but his style was different. Perhaps some of his unconventionality was rooted in the fact that he was not financially dependent on the U.S. Army. He was independently wealthy and could have enjoyed the life of a well-to-do sportsman had he been so inclined. On another level, however, he needed the army and was convinced that the army needed him. He had a mystical streak and believed that the entity of which George Patton was the latest manifestation had been reincarnated through the ages, always as a soldier for a particular purpose.

He graduated from West Point as a cavalry officer—he would win many trophies for horsemanship—but during World War I was attached to the fledgling tank corps after serving on General Pershing's staff. Patton then led the 304th Light Tank Brigade in the St. Mihiel offensive and was wounded on the first day of the Argonne campaign. He ended the war as a colonel, but, like most of his fellow officers, he had to revert to his peacetime rank of captain. By 1920, he was promoted to major and spent fourteen years in that rank.

Between the world wars, Patton and Eisenhower formed a firm friendship. Despite his ego and his seniority

1–4. Lt. Gen. George S. Patton Jr. (*standing*), Third Army, addresses the officers of the 80th Infantry Division at Ville-au-Val, France, in November 1944. Maj. Gen. Manton S. Eddy, XII Corps commander, sits at left, with Maj. Gen. Horace L. McBride at right.

to Ike, Patton seems to have believed that Ike was his natural superior. He is said to have commented that, in any future war, Ike would be the army's Gen. Robert E. Lee; Patton, the Stonewall Jackson. By 1941, Patton had attained command of the 2d Armored Division, later of the I Armored Corps. His first action in World War II was in North Africa as leader of the II Corps. Returning to England after the Sicily campaign, he assumed command of the Third Army.

Although Patton's highly emotional nature was nearly his undoing, his relentless drive and talent for extracting the impossible from his men made him invaluable. It was not entirely out of friendship that Eisenhower kept Patton in position, even after chastising him severely. While acknowledging Patton was not a strategist, Ike knew that he was a superb tactician and possessed a most rare talent— the ability and will to pursue. Ike had studied enough combat history to know how many battles had been lost through the failure to pursue.

One of Patton's corps commanders was Maj. Gen. John Millikin (1–5). His III Corps would relieve Bastogne as part of the Third Army's amazing swing north.

Maj. Gen. Troy H. ("Troop") Middleton (1–6) was a rare bird among the top brass in that he once temporarily gave up on the army. During World War I, he had served as a colonel in the infantry and, with the coming of peace, had to take the usual cut in rank with the equally usual slim chances of advancement. He stuck it out until he had

accumulated twenty-nine years of service and then retired in 1937. One of his peacetime stations had been as a professor of military science and tactics at Louisiana State University. Upon retirement, he returned to that institution as the dean of administration.

With World War II, he was recalled to active duty and rapidly rose to command the 45th Infantry Division in Sicily. There he sustained a knee injury serious enough to send him stateside to Walter Reed Army Hospital. Eisenhower learned of Middleton's whereabouts from Marshall, and Ike asked that Middleton be returned to Europe. According to Ike's son John, the general remarked, "I would rather have Troop Middleton commanding VIII Corps from a stretcher than anyone else I know in perfect health."

Another of Patton's corps commanders involved in the major realignment north was Maj. Gen. Manton S. Eddy (1–7). It was one of Eddy's units that would effect Patton's first crossing of the Rhine on 23 March 1945.

From the British evacuation at Dunkirk until roughly D-Day, most of the Allied action in western Europe had been by air. The more ardent advocates of airpower hoped that strategic bombing could so devastate Germany as to force its surrender and make unnecessary the immense loss of life inherent in a ground invasion. For all the damage the air forces inflicted, however, they had not forced Germany to sue for peace. By dispersing some industries, maintaining horrendous work hours, and sharply cutting

1-5. Maj. Gen. John Millikin, III Corps, poses for a photographer at Fort McPherson, Georgia, on 13 November 1943.

1-6. Maj. Gen. Troy H. Middleton, VIII Corps, shown here 10 July 1943 aboard USS *Ancon* (AGC-4) while that ship was engaged in landing operations off Scoglitti, Sicily.

1-7. Major General Eddy, XII Corps (then commanding the 9th Infantry Division), visiting the front in Tunisia on 8 May 1943.

items for civilian consumption, Germany not only kept going but achieved a wartime high in ordnance production in the autumn of 1944. With the invasion of the continent, the overall mission of the U.S. Army Air Force (USAAF) and the Royal Air Force (RAF) was to support the widespread and heavy ground forces. Each service was indispensable, for alone neither airpower nor ground troops could achieve victory.

In overall command of the USAAF was Gen. Carl A. ("Tooey") Spaatz (1–8). A West Point graduate in 1914, he served in World War I as a fighter pilot. In 1929, he and then-Capt. Ira C. Eaker established an aircraft endurance record for which they received the Distinguished Flying Cross. By 1941, he was in the office of the chief of the Air Staff, where he unsuccessfully recommended a separate air force. With the advent of World War II, his rise was rapid. He commanded, in turn, the Air Combat Command, the Eighth Air Force, and the Northwest African Strategic Air Force. In 1944, he became chief of the U.S. Strategic Air Forces in Europe. After the war, he became head of the USSAFE.

To the general public, probably the most easily recognizable name of any of Spaatz's subordinates was that of Lt. Gen. James H. ("Jimmie") Doolittle (1–9). He had enlisted as a flying cadet in 1917 and was a second lieutenant in World War I. After the war, he established several air records, including being the first to fly across the United States in less than twenty-four hours. He received a doctorate from the Massachusetts Institute of Technology in 1925. Five years later, he went off active duty and returned as a major in 1940. He became a public hero on

1-8. Gen. Carl A. Spaatz, U.S. Strategic Air Forces in Europe.

1-9. Lt. Gen. James H. Doolittle, Eighth Air Force (Strategic).

1-10. Lt. Gen. Hoyt S. Vandenberg, Ninth Air Force.

1-11. Maj. Gen. Samuel E. Anderson, IX Bombardment Division.

18 April 1942, when, as a lieutenant colonel, he led the first air raid on Tokyo and other Japanese cities. Soon a brigadier general, he took command of the Northwest African Strategic Air Force. In 1944, he commanded the Fifteenth Air Force and later the Eighth Air Force.

Lt. Gen. Hoyt S. Vandenberg (1–10) had joined the air corps in 1923. Early on he demonstrated the intelligence and charisma that would eventually take him to the top. During World War II he served in such spots as chief of staff, Northwest African Strategic Air Force; head of an air mission to Russia; and command of the Ninth Air Force. After the war he would be in charge of military intelligence at the War Department General Staff and then would leave active duty to head the Central Intelligence Agency (CIA). He returned to active duty in April 1948 to replace Spaatz as chief of staff of the U.S. Air Force (USAF).

Maj. Gen. Samuel E. Anderson (1–11) was another World War II commander who enjoyed a distinguished postwar career. He rose to full general and headed the USAF Research and Development Command and the Air Matériel Command.

Maj. Gen. Paul L. Williams (1–12) was in charge of C-47s flying out of England. His group would play a major role in keeping Bastogne's isolated garrison supplied during the bleak days of late December 1944.

At forty years of age, Maj. Gen. Elwood L. ("Pete") Quesada (1–13) was the youngest general officer in the European theater. In 1942 he was a lieutenant colonel but ended the war as a major general. He served in Africa in 1943 and in the invasion of Italy. Early in 1944, he became a major general and head of the IX Tactical Air Command. Quesada could well be considered the father of the Tactical Air Command.

1-12. Maj. Gen. Paul L. Williams, IX Troop Carrier Command.

1-13. Maj. Gen. Elwood L. Quesada, IX Tactical Air Command, supporting Hodges's First Army, (left) with Lt. Gen. Bradley.

Maj. Gen. Otto P. Weyland (1–14) came to the service from Texas A&M in 1923. His career followed the usual course of service schools and assignments, and he so proved his worth that he became a brigadier general in 1943. He was closely associated with tactical air power and, as a full general in 1952, headed the Tactical Air Command.

1-14. Maj. Gen. Otto P. Weyland, XIX Tactical Air Command, supporting Patton's Third Army.

THE GERMAN LEADERS

By late September 1944 when Adolf Hitler (1–15) gathered with his top brass and announced his decision to attack through the Ardennes, the Führer was a sick man. The attempted assassination that summer had left him with periodic twitches in his right arm, and his recurring dizzy spells and splitting headaches may have also been exacerbated by that incident. The medication he was taking worsened rather than helped his painful stomach ailment. He looked older than his fifty-four years, and that morning he had suffered what was probably a slight heart attack. But he was still as dangerous as a wolf.

Generalfeldmarschall Wilhelm Keitel (1–16) was Hitler's longtime favorite and was absolutely loyal to him. Not one of the brightest men in Hitler's entourage, by late 1944 Keitel had lost much of his prestige and influence over the prosecution of the war. He did, however, make a significant impact on the Ardennes Offensive through his staff work, particularly in the area of logistical planning.

Just as devoted to Hitler as Keitel but much more intelligent, Generaloberst Alfred Jodl (1–17) had a strong personality that he soft-pedaled in favor of the Führer. His strong point was operational plans; thus, Hitler entrusted him with studying the feasibility of the Ardennes campaign.

1-15. Adolf Hitler, Führer of the German Reich, shown during Benito Mussolini's visit on 25 July 1944 and shortly after the attempt on Hitler's life.

1-16. Generalfeldmarschall Wilhelm Keitel, chief of *Oberkommando Wehrmacht* (OKW), chats with Joseph Goebbels and Martin Bormann.

1-17.   Generaloberst Alfred Jodl, chief of staff
of the German Army (center), briefs Hitler
and Hermann Fegelein (Eva Braun's
brother-in-law).

1-18.   Generalfeldmarschall Gerd von Rundstedt
(*left*), *Oberbefehlshaber West* in mid-1944,
accompanied by his then–chief of staff
Generalleutnant Günther Blumentritt (*right*).

A very different type was Generalfeldmarschall Gerd
von Rundstedt (1–18), an aristocrat and gentleman to his
fingertips—urbane, affable, and courtly. Naturally Hitler
disliked him, and Rundstedt reciprocated the sentiment.
The latter was not a Nazi, but he was bound by his honor
as a soldier to serve the Fatherland, whoever was at the
helm. His wit could be stinging, and sometimes he treated
his trusted associates to acid comments about history, pol-
itics, and the officers close to Hitler. Nevertheless, Hitler
needed Rundstedt, if only as a figurehead, because the old
soldier was a prime favorite with the German people.

Hitler referred to Generalfeldmarschall Walter Model

(1–19) as his best field marshal. Certainly he was one of
the most interesting. The son of a schoolteacher, Model
was deeply devoted to his country and to the army. His
colleagues considered him a very energetic commander
and a brilliant tactician. Known more as a master of defense than of offense, nevertheless he set great store by
originality. Model could drive his officers to the brink, but
he had a good rapport with his enlisted men. He was a
completely dedicated soldier, with few friends and little
social life, and he was a devoted Christian and family
man.

Model had a good background in armor, having commanded the 3. Panzer-Division in Russia during the 1941
battles of the Bialystok-Minsk pocket and the crossing of

1-19.   Adolf Hitler greets
Generalfeldmarschall
Walter Model,
commander of
Heeresgruppe B during
the Ardennes Offensive.

1–20. General der Panzertruppen Hasso von Manteuffel, 5. Panzer-Armee. Note the two cuff titles on his tunic, *Afrika* and *Grossdeutschland*.

the Dnieper River. Given command of the 9. Armee in 1942, Model stayed in that position until January 1944, when he took command of Army Group North on the Eastern Front. In March 1944, he advanced to General-feldmarschall, commanded various army groups in the east, and later even served a brief stint with *Oberbefehlshaber West (OB West)*. Ultimately, Model took command of Heeresgruppe B in September 1944 and retained the post until his suicide in April 1945, after the army to which he had devoted his professional energies disintegrated.

No one spotting General der Panzertruppen Hasso von Manteuffel (1–20) out of uniform would have pigeonholed him as a German general. His height has been estimated at five feet, three inches, his weight, 120 pounds. The youngest of Model's army commanders, the Prussian-born Manteuffel was by training a cavalry officer. By the war's end, he was one of Germany's most highly decorated soldiers.

If his fitness reports were any indication, he was exceptional. He possessed the type of decisive, analytical mind needed to evaluate fluid situations and act accordingly. Manteuffel commanded a *Panzergrenadier* regiment during the heady days of the initial drive into Russia in 1941. By November 1942, he was a division commander under Generalfeldmarschall Erwin Rommel in Tunisia. Evacuated to Europe in 1943, he went on to command the 7. Panzer-Division and the Panzergrenadier-Division *Grossdeutschland* in 1944. His stellar performance in the east caused Hitler to elevate him from divisional command, past the corps level, to lead the 5. Panzer-Armee in September 1944.

One of Manteuffel's subordinates was General der Panzertruppen Heinrich von Lüttwitz (1–21). He had started his career as an enlisted man, volunteering for service in 1914. In less than a year, he had been com-

missioned and, as Manteuffel, became a cavalry officer. A contemporary described him as "a passionate soldier" who led his men "by his personality." While not a brilliant strategist, his extensive combat experience gave him a deep understanding of the capabilities and limitations of the average German soldier.

Lüttwitz brought with him a solid background in tanks and armored strategy. Over the span of three years in the east, he commanded the 2. and the 20. Panzer divisions before being elevated to corps command.

1–21. General der Panzertruppen Heinrich von Lüttwitz, XLVII. Panzerkorps.

1–22. General der Artillerie Walter Lucht, LXVI Armeekorps.

1–23. General der Panzertruppen Walter Krüger, LVIII. Panzerkorps

1–24. SS-Oberstgruppenführer Josef Dietrich, 6. Panzer-Armee, at Berchtesgaden, while commander of the 1. SS-Panzer-Division. On his right pocket hangs the ribbon of the Blood Order, a medal struck for participants in Hitler's 1923 Beer Hall Putsch. (Photo by Eva Braun)

Another solid leader was General der Artillerie Walter Lucht (1–22). He brought to the offensive a background in artillery and experience derived from the Eastern Front, having been chief of artillery within the 336. Infanterie-Division during 1941 and 1942. Afterward, he led his division during the Second Battle of Kharkov and in the unsuccessful effort to relieve his besieged comrades at Stalingrad.

Promoted to General der Panzertruppen, Walter Krüger (1–23) shared a common background in armor with his fellow in command of the 1. Panzer-Division. After promotion to full general in May 1944, Krüger took over the LVIII. Panzerkorps, which he would lead in the Ardennes Offensive.

Perhaps the weakest of Model's army commanders, SS-Oberstgruppenführer Josef ("Sepp") Dietrich (1–24) was a longtime Nazi and personal friend of Adolf Hitler, for whom he had been a chauffeur and bodyguard in 1928. Dietrich was fortunate to be so close to Hitler, as his blunt, outspoken character could have landed him in front of a firing squad. At times he took advantage of Hitler's tolerance to defend his fellow officers.

Dietrich was something of a paradox among his peers, many of whom despised him. Some regarded him as a master of small unit maneuver, and others, in Rundstedt's words, saw Dietrich as "decent but stupid." Dietrich did, however, bring a wealth of experience to the offensive, as he had led the 1. SS-Panzer-Division *Leibstandarte Adolf Hitler* (Adolf Hitler Bodyguard) from its inception until he took over leadership of the I. SS-Panzerkorps in July 1943. One year later, he was elevated to command the 6. Panzer-Armee. Although he played a relatively minor role in the Ardennes campaign, later Rundstedt held him responsible for certain errors at critical junctures during the

offensive, and the Allies held him accountable for the Malmédy massacre.

Both of Dietrich's armored corps commanders had extensive experience commanding armor on the Eastern Front. SS-Gruppenführer Hermann Priess (1–25) led the 3. SS-Panzer-Division *Totenkopf* (Death's Head) in Russia from 10 October 1943 until 20 June 1944. On 24 October 1944, Priess assumed command of the I. SS-Panzerkorps, a post he held until the war's end.

1–25. SS-Gruppenführer Hermann Priess, I. SS-Panzerkorps.

1-26. SS-Obergruppenführer Willi Bittrich, II. SS-Panzerkorps, shown here as an Oberführer.

1-27. Generalleutnant Otto Hitzfeld, LXVII. Korps.

1-28. General der Panzertruppen Erich Brandenburger, 7. Armee.

SS-Obergruppenführer Willi Bittrich (1–26) certainly had the most varied career of any of Dietrich's corps-level commanders. He started as a *Luftwaffe* (air force) officer but opted for transfer to the *Waffen-SS,* ostensibly to take advantage of the reputed rapid pace of promotion in that organization.

His gamble paid off. He advanced quickly, ultimately assuming temporary command of the 2. SS-Panzer-Division *Das Reich* for three months in 1941. In the following three years, he led in succession the 8. SS-Kavallerie-Division-*Florian Geyer* and the 9. SS-Panzer-Division *Hohenstaufen.* He was promoted to Obergruppenführer shortly after taking command of the II. SS-Panzerkorps on 10 July 1944. Bittrich is best remembered for his corps's destruction of the British 1st Airborne Division's bridgehead at Arnhem.

Dietrich's two SS-Panzerkorps were supported by the LXVII. Armeekorps, commanded by Generalleutnant Otto Hitzfeld (1–27). With a solid background in commanding infantry in support of armor. Hitzfeld had led the 102. Infanterie-Division during most of 1943 as a part of the XXXIX. Panzerkorps.

Compared with Manteuffel and Dietrich, General der Panzertruppen Erich Brandenburger (1–28) was the least favorite of Model's three army commanders. Moreover, it was common knowledge that Model disliked Brandenburger, who was a product of the general staff system. Manteuffel said Brandenburger had the "features of a scientist," hardly an attribute that would appeal to the relentless, hard-driving Model. Brandenburger stood in stark contrast to Dietrich, who followed his heart rather than his head and who always seemed to be spoiling for a brawl.

Nonetheless, Brandenburger brought with him a wealth of experience to justify his being entrusted with the command of an army. From 1941 through 1943, he led the 8. Panzer-Division, part of General Erich von Manstein's LVI. Panzerkorps, and took part in the 1941 battles of Kvinski, Luga, Lake Ilmen, and Novgorod. The defensive battles of Army Group Center occupied Brandenburger's division during 1942. Following promotion to General der Panzertruppen in August 1943, he led the XXIX. Armeekorps for a year before taking over the 7. Armee.

From the credentials of General der Kavallerie Edwin von Rothkirch (1–29), it could be argued that he was the least qualified of the nine corps commanders to take part in a major offensive. Most of his experience early in the war had been limited to commanding Breslau's fortifications and the occupation forces of Lvov.

1-29. General der Kavallerie Edwin von Rothkirch, LIII. Korps.

1-30. General der Infanterie Franz Beyer, LXXX. Korps.

Rothkirch did command the 9. Armee's 330. Infanterie-Division in the heavy defensive fighting of 1942–43, but then he reverted to guarding the German lines of communication in White Russia in 1944. Rothkirch then commanded LIII. Korps from 1944 until he was captured by the Americans in March 1945.

Silesian-born like Rothkirch, General der Infanterie Franz Beyer (1–30) had more in the way of field command experience, having led the 331. Infanterie-Division in the defensive fighting of 1942–43 and taking over the 44. Infanterie-Division in Italy in 1944. That year also

found Beyer promoted to General der Infanterie and to corps command.

Commanding Brandenburger's LXXXV. Korps was General der Infanterie Baptist Kniess (not pictured). His 215. Infanterie-Division played a minor role during the invasion of France and was posted there until the late 1941 crisis on the Eastern Front. Then, attached to Army Group North, the 215. fought in the battle of Volkhov south of Leningrad from January through March 1942. Kniess advanced to corps command and took over the LXVI. Korps in November 1942.

Though Reichsmarschall Herman Göring (1–31) was still close to Hitler and a popular figure in Germany, his stature had diminished by late 1944. His fliers' morale was flagging in the face of fatigue and overwhelming odds, not to mention Göring's unremitting criticisms and charges of cowardice. His legacy was devolving into a string of broken promises—first, to crush the RAF following the invasion of France, then to supply the surrounded 6. Armee at Stalingrad, and finally to turn back the Allied bomber offensive. Now he was making yet another promise to provide unrealistic numbers of aircraft and pilots in support of the Ardennes Offensive.

Following the invasion of Normandy, the role of the German fighter arm inevitably evolved into a support role for the *Wehrmacht*'s ground forces. When planning for the Ardennes Offensive, only two *Jagdgeschwader* (fighter groups) were still fighting in defense of the Reich. All of the ten fighter groups originally sent from the interior and now operating with the troops on the Western Front were now under the overall command of Generalleutnant Josef Schmidt (1–32).

1-31. Reichsmarschall Hermann Göring, *Luftwaffe* commander in chief (*center right*), on the occasion of the Führer's birthday on 20 April 1944.

1–32. Generalleutnant Josef Schmidt, Luftwaffen-Kommando West.

1–33. Generalleutnant and Inspekteur der Jagdflieger Adolf Galland (*left*), commander of the *Luftwaffe* day fighters, confers with Hitler at the Wolf's Lair in East Prussia.

One of Hitler's favorites during the Battle of Britain and afterward, Generalleutnant (Inspekteur der Jagdflieger) Adolf Galland (1–33) had gradually lost influence over how the air war was conducted. This was partly due to the *Luftwaffe*'s inability to stem the Allied bombing offensive and protect Germany's industrial cities and partly due to Galland's vehement disagreement with Hitler over the development of the Messerschmitt Me-262 Schwalbe (Swallow) jet fighter.

Galland saw Operation *Bodenplatte* ("Baseplate"—the *Luftwaffe*'s mission to support the Ardennes Offensive by destroying the Allied air forces on the ground) as a gigantic gamble with Germany's last reserves of fighter aircraft and pilots—reserves that would be desperately needed to repel the inevitable final assault on the German homeland. Ironically, after presiding over the virtual destruction of his beloved fighter arm, Galland was relieved in the wake of the offensive and placed in command of JV-44, the world's first jet fighter group.

CHAPTER 2

Men and Machines

GERMAN DIVISIONAL STRUCTURE

Necessary to evaluating the apparent strength of the German order of battle for the Ardennes Offensive is a basic understanding of the German infantry division's transformation from 1943 to late 1944 (2–1). In October 1943, the Germans radically reorganized their infantry divisions, whereby the number of rifle battalions within each of the three regiments decreased from three to two. The number of squads in each rifle platoon went from four to three, and the trains at all levels were reduced. In an effort to maintain the total firepower of the divisions, the calibers of the mortars and antitank guns were increased.

In September 1944, the German infantry division was once again transformed, this time into the *Volksgrenadier* division, or "Peoples' Infantry Division," so designated to stress the state of emergency that the Fatherland faced. Additional decreases in personnel were ordered, however, but were offset to a degree by increasing the number of automatic weapons. Company trains and logistical support were consolidated into battalion supply platoons, freeing the company-level commanders from all but operational concerns.

The most significant change in the newly organized *Volksgrenadier* divisions was the caliber of the men in the rank and file. As the burned-out, often virtually destroyed divisions returned from the Eastern Front meat grinder for rebuilding, rear areas were swept clean of what were considered unnecessary support troops. These men were then channeled into the *Volksgrenadier* divisions. The young, the middle-aged, and the somewhat infirm were drafted and lumped together with miscellaneous troops from the various services in a conglomeration from which any degree of unit cohesion and esprit de corps could hardly have been expected. Thus, the quality of these infantry di-

visions was uneven. Some were quite good and fought well, having been formed around cadres of veterans from the campaigns in Russia. Others, however, were little better than armed mobs.

In contrast to the *Volksgrenadier* divisions were the *Panzer* divisions, particularly those of the *Waffen-SS,* which, at least from a manpower standpoint, were generally at full strength. Germany tended to funnel the better, more highly motivated recruits into these divisions. However well staffed the armored divisions tended to be, though, the units were unable to re-equip themselves fully before the Ardennes Offensive. Germany was simply unable to replace the immense losses in matériel suffered on the Eastern Front and in Normandy.

Each German *Panzer* division was composed of a single tank regiment, supported by two *Panzergrenadier,* or armored infantry, regiments. Even with *Panzerjäger* (tank destroyer) and *Sturmgeschütz* (assault gun) battalions attached, a typical *Panzer* division was outgunned if not outmanned by its U.S. counterpart.

A *Panzer* regiment comprised two tank battalions of four companies each. The latest equipment tended to be concentrated in the lead battalion, while older tanks and assault guns rounded out the complement of vehicles in the second battalion.

EQUIPMENT OF THE GERMAN FOOT SOLDIER

The Mauser Kar 98k was the basic weapon of the German infantryman. German automatic-rifle development never progressed to the point where the production of these bolt-action rifles could cease. The example in photo 2–2 is a

2–1: COMPARISON OF 1939–1943 INFANTRY DIVISION AND *VOLKSGRENADIER* DIVISION

	Personnel Strength		Machine-Gun Strength*		Mortar/ Bazooka Strength		Artillery Strength		Motor Vehicle Strength	
	39–43 Div.	*Volks.* Div.	39–43 Div.	*Volks.* Div.	39–43 Div.	*Volks.* Div.	39–43 Div.	*Volks.* Div.	39–43 Div.	*Volks.* Div.
Divisional HQ	158	227	2	17	—	—	—	—	31	32
Fusilier Co.	—	200	—	94	—	2	—	2	—	—
Recon. Btn.	625	—	33	—	—	—	2	—	30	—
Signal Btn.	474	305	17	16	—	—	—	—	103	44
Infantry Rgt. #1	3,250	1,911	159	692	45	92	8	12	73	10
Infantry Rgt. #2	3,250	1,854	159	692	45	92	8	12	73	9
Infantry Rgt. #3	3,250	1,854	159	692	45	92	8	12	73	9
Artillery Rgt.	2,500	1,744	32	177	—	—	48	54	105	99
Antitank Btn.	550	460	18	56	—	—	—	—	114	100
Engineer Btn.	843	442	34	33	—	4	—	—	87	12
Supply Rgt.	—	1,075	—	18	—	—	—	—	—	111
Div. Services	2,300	—	30	—	—	—	—	—	253	—
Total	17,200	10,072	643	2,487	142	282	74	92	942	426

* All types, including submachine guns

2-2. Mauser Kar 98k rifle.

production variation where the butt plate enclosed the rifle butt to a depth of about one-half inch. The small circular disk on the lower stock is to strengthen the stock.

Often touted as the "trademark of the *Wehrmacht*" (2–3), the MP40's design maximized the use of simple machine-press stampings. Very light, durable, and easy to produce, its chief drawback was its comparatively small magazine capacity of thirty rounds.

Accepted as the standard assault rifle of the *Wehrmacht* was the Sturmgewehr StG44 (assault rifle, model 1944) (2–4). Variably designated the MP43, it was easily manufactured, rugged, seemingly impervious to the elements, and a great favorite with the German troops. This weapon held a thirty-round magazine.

Growing out of the *Luftwaffe*'s desire for a compact paratrooper rifle that used the standard, full-sized 7.92mm round, the FG42 (2–5) was an effective, high-powered weapon. The heavy recoil of its larger cartridge, however, made it difficult to shoot accurately.

2-3. American soldiers examine a captured Schmeisser MP40 machine pistol.

2–4. Pvt. Henry R. Riggan cleans a captured German Sturmgewehr 44 (StG44); note MG42 in foreground.

One of the most feared weapons in the German arsenal was the MG42 machine gun (2–6). Because of its ruggedness and reliability, it was the weapon of choice for the *Wehrmacht.* Its incredible firing rate—nearly twenty rounds per second—made it a most fearsome weapon. The barrel could be changed (recommended every 250 rounds) in the field in five seconds.

The Stielhandgranate 39 (2–7) was practically another trademark of the German soldier. This grenade was charged by first unscrewing a protective metal cap at the lower end of the handle and then by pulling a porcelain bead attached to a silk cord. This action initiated a friction primer that detonated the seven-ounce TNT charge after a four-and-one-half second delay. By using a trip wire, the StiGr39 could also serve as a booby trap and even as an antitank device. In the latter case, six grenades were lashed together, with the grenade in the center acting as a detonator.

Photo 2–8 illustrates items associated with the German soldier. Bearing the army national insignia, his helmet weighed an average of 2.2 pounds, depending on its size. American cigarettes were much prized. The *Soldbuch,* or paybook, was the German soldier's official means of identification. In addition to listing such items as promotions, inoculations, and clothing and equipment issues, the *Soldbuch* contained a record of all units in which an indi-

2–5. Fallschirmjägergewehr 42 (FG42) paratrooper rifle.

2–6. The MG42 machine gun.

2-7. Lieutenant Dreyden, U.S. Army Engineers, demonstrates the charging mechanism of a German Stielhandgranate 39 high-explosive stick grenade, or "potato masher."

2-8. Personal items and equipment frequently handled and associated with the German soldier—his helmet, bayonet, cigarettes, and *Soldbuch*.

vidual had served, making it a most valuable piece of intelligence in the event of his capture.

Popular images of clean-cut, jackbooted soldiers on parade after the capture of Paris bore little resemblance to the German infantrymen of late 1944. The wool uniforms issued by this time had a high rayon content, wore out quickly, and lost their shape in the first rain. Moreover, by

this time many German soldiers were wearing camouflage clothing (2–9). Much of the clothing was reversible to white, a feature often utilized during the Ardennes Offensive. The soldier on the left in photo 2–10 wears a camouflage parka over a standard field-gray tunic, while the helmeted man at right dons an overcoat. Note the mess kit dangling from his belt.

2-9. The 200,000th German POW captured by the Third Army wears a camouflaged parka, reversible to white.

2-10. Captured German soldiers in December 1944 display the variety of clothing worn by the rank and file.

GERMAN TANKS, OTHER VEHICLES, AND WEAPONS

The Germans possessed three main battle tanks: Panzer-kampfwagen (PzKpfw) IV, PzKpfw V Panther, and two variants of the PzKpfw VI Tiger. Having earned the status of "workhorse tank" after many a campaign prior to the Ardennes Offensive, by late 1944 the PzKpfw IV (2–11) was obsolescent and was being replaced in substantial numbers by the PzKpfw V Panther. The PzKpfw IV was still a mainstay, however. It comprised 43 percent of Germany's tank strength, with a total of 274 vehicles spread evenly throughout the armored divisions poised for the offensive. Its main armament, the 75mm L/48 gun, was highly effective and much superior to its U.S. counterpart on the Sherman tank. The PzKpfw IV's chief drawback was its light armor, which was insufficiently sloped on the chassis and turret.

The Panther (2–12) was arguably one of the best tanks of World War II. It was easily distinguishable from the PzKpfw IV by virtue of its eight pairs of large road wheels and its taller, sloped turret. Improvements over its predecessor included the 75mm L/70 high-velocity gun and a higher maximum road speed of 29 miles per hour. Draw-

2–11. Panzerkampfwagen IV medium tank.

backs were its ponderous forty-five tons and rather poor fuel efficiency, but its heavy armor made it almost invulnerable to frontal attack. The Panther was a great favorite of the *Panzer* crews and numbered 54 percent, or about 344 vehicles, of the total tank strength in the Ardennes as of 10 December 1944.

2–12. Panzerkampfwagen V Panther heavy medium tank.

2–13. Panzerkampfwagen VI Ausf. E Tiger I heavy tank.

Although similar in overall dimensions to the Panther and mounting a comparable chassis, the Tiger I (2–13) featured still heavier armor and the 88mm L/56 gun, which the American tankers dreaded. Visually, the turret was similar to that of the PzKpfw IV, but the Tiger was easily recognized because of its immense size and large road wheels. The Tigers were greatly feared, but their heavy armor piled yet more weight (twelve additional tons) onto the vehicle, limiting its maneuverability and top speed (24 miles per hour). A relatively small number of Tiger Is—perhaps twenty—took part in the offensive.

The Tiger II, or *Königstiger* (King Tiger), (2–14) was designed to mount the longer 88mm L/71 gun. A turret very similar in appearance to that of the Panther accommodated this improvement. The weight of the vehicle, however, rose to a staggering sixty-eight tons, reducing its top speed to 21 miles per hour. The ponderous mass of the King Tigers often forced the Germans to bypass poor, unpaved roads and flimsy bridges. Even with mechanical

improvements, the Tiger IIs proved unreliable and were prone to break down. The greatest drawback to the Tiger variants—and the Panther to a lesser degree—was that they were voracious gas-guzzlers, creating supply problems for the already fuel-starved *Panzer* divisions. Perhaps fifty Tiger IIs participated in the offensive. All were assigned to the *schwere Panzer-Abteilungen* (heavy tank battalions) of the various armored divisions.

In addition to tanks, the *Panzer* divisions' inventory contained a number of assault gun and tank destroyer vehicles. The assault gun also functioned as the primary fighting vehicle of the *Panzergrenadier* divisions. Built on a tank chassis, they were constructed without a turret, mounting a large-caliber gun semi-fixed forward. As the vehicle had to be pointed in the direction it was going to shoot, its aiming ability was limited. A total of about 289 assault guns of various types were marshaled in the Ardennes on 10 December 1944. In photo 2–15, a captured StuG III mounting a 75mm L/48 gun sits in the road near Inden, Germany, in December 1944.

2–14. Panzerkampfwagen VI Ausf. B Tiger II heavy tank.

2–15. Sturmgeschütz III assault gun.

2–16. A snow-covered, wrecked Jagdpanzer IV off the side of a road near Cherain, Belgium.

The Germans termed their tank destroyers (2–16) *Jagdpanzer,* or "hunting tanks." Their characteristics included low silhouettes and semi-fixed, forward-firing guns.

Due to the chronic shortage of armor, the Germans made use of American vehicles whenever possible and whenever they were in running shape. The Germans captured the Sherman tank shown in photo 2–17 from the 10th Armored Division. This same division later knocked it out and recaptured it. Note the missing turret and, on the side, that the American star has been painted out.

Frequently used with other motorcycles at the head of an armored column, the Kettenkraftrad SdKfz 2 (2–18) was particularly useful on the muddy roads of the Ardennes. The German abbreviation SdKfz stands for *Sonder-Kraftfahrzeug,* or "special-purpose motor vehicle."

Used as a light personnel carrier, the Kübelwagen (bucket car) was a familiar sight in the Ardennes. The example here (2–19) is a prize captured in North Africa, as evidenced by the *Afrika Korps* insignia on the passenger

door. During tests in February 1943 at the Aberdeen Proving Ground in Maryland, the German vehicle failed to compare favorably with its U.S. counterpart, the Willys/Ford jeep. Not only were the Kübelwagen's performance characteristics less efficient, but it was also prone to break down in the field.

2–18. SdKfz 2 Kettenkraftrad, or half-tracked motorcycle.

2–17. A captured U.S. tank impressed into German service.

2–19. Volkswagen Typ 82, Kfz 1 Kübelwagen (*right*) and an American jeep.

2-20. Zugkraftwagen 8t SdKfz 7 medium semi-tracked vehicle, or prime mover. The "8t" refers to its 8-ton capacity.

mount an assortment of guns on the chassis of the vehicle itself.

Apart from prime movers, the *Wehrmacht* had two primary personnel carriers—the SdKfz 251 medium and SdKfz 250 light—that were both armored half-tracks. The SdKfz 251, the primary armored personnel carrier (APC), had a crew of two and could carry either ten passengers or mount a wide assortment of equipment and arms. It even served as an armored ambulance. The smaller SdKfz 250 light APC was employed primarily in the *Aufklärungs,* or reconnaissance, units.

The best antitank gun in the German arsenal was the famous "Eighty-eight," the 88mm Pak (Panzerabwehrkanone), a weapon that among the apprehensive Allies enjoyed almost mythical destructive power. Actually, the 88mm Pak could stop any armored vehicle that the Americans could put on the road. Its main drawback is that there were not enough of them. Shown in 2–21 is the Pak 43/41 variant.

The 75mm Pak 40 (2–22) was likely the most numerous of the German antitank guns. Although a very effective weapon, its crews would have preferred having the much-feared, powerful Pak 43/41.

Though classed as medium vehicles, prime movers weighed from three to eighteen tons and were the workhorses of the armored division (2–20). Some were used as personnel carriers, although their main function was to act as a tow for artillery. In addition, prime movers could

2-21. 88mm Pak 43/41.

2-22. 75mm Pak 40 antitank gun.

Because of shortages, the *Wehrmacht* had to improvise in many areas, including its antitank guns. The 75mm Pak 97/38 (2–23) employed the French 75mm model 1897 gun on a 50mm Pak 38 carriage.

The 105mm K18 medium gun (2–24) provided the German divisional field artillery's long-range punch. But the bulk of the field artillery assigned to the German divisions were the 105mm M18 leFH howitzers (2–25) of World War I vintage. In 1941, they were retrofitted with muzzle brakes to enable them to fire a new long-range charge. "leFH" is an abbreviation for leichte Feld-Haubitze (light field howitzer). A further modification of the model 1918 field howitzer, the 105mm leFH 18/40 (2–26) was mounted on a 75mm Pak 40 carriage.

The Germans hoped that the execrable winter weather conditions might preclude a display of U.S. airpower. Still, Flak (Flugabwehr-Kanonen, or "antiaircraft gun"), regiments and battalions (2–27) were allotted to each of the German corps and divisions to shoulder the burden of protecting the advancing Heeresgruppe B columns.

2–23. 75mm Pak 97/38 antitank gun with a Solothurn perforated muzzle brake.

2–24. 105mm K.18 medium gun.

2–25. 105mm leFH 18 howitzer.

In addition to field artillery attached at the corps and division level, the typical German corps had a *Werfer* (rocket-launcher) brigade composed of two regiments and equipped with six-tubed 150mm launchers (2–28). To escape the blast during launch, the crew took shelter in a slit trench some fifteen yards out on either flank. The Nebelwerfer was fired electrically, with the six tubes discharging in sequence within ten seconds.

The equivalent of the U.S. 81mm mortar M1, the 80mm Granatwerfer 34 (2–29) was standard equipment in the heavy-weapons company of every German infantry battalion. A trained crew could fire the mortar at a rate of twelve rounds per minute. Used primarily as a close-range weapon, the Granatwerfer's range was just short of six hundred yards, although it could be extended incrementally to twenty-five hundred yards with a series of four additional propellant charges.

2-26. 105mm leFH 18/40 howitzer.

2-27. 88mm Flak 36 mobile antiaircraft gun.

2-28. Nebelwerfer 41 150mm rocket launcher.

2-29. Schwerer Granatwerfer 34 80mm medium mortar.

2–30. James J. Ballas inspects a captured German Panzerfaust 44mm recoilless antitank grenade launcher.

2–31. Panzerfaust rocket-propelled projectile with tail assembly.

88mm Raketenpanzerbüchse 54, or Panzerschreck, demonstrated by two American soldiers in St.-Mère-Église, France.

2–33. Tellermine 42 antitank mine.

The Panzerfaust, or "tank fist," was a one-shot antitank bazooka in wide use on both the Eastern and Western fronts, particularly late in the war. The weapon consisted of a steel tube containing the sight and trigger mechanism. A rocket-propelled projectile with a hollow-head charge was placed in and fired from the forward portion of the tube, which was then discarded. The soldier in photo 2–30 demonstrates how to insert the projectile. The red stenciling reads "Vorsicht! Starker Feuerstrahl!" [Caution! Strong flame jet!]

When the Panzerfaust was fired, spring-loaded fins on the projectile folded out to stabilize the warhead on its way to the target (2–31). In the hands of a determined infantryman working at a range of thirty to eighty meters, the Panzerfaust was more than a match for any Allied armored vehicle.

The Germans developed the Panzerschreck (tank terror) from a captured U.S. M1 2.36-inch rocket launcher, and it was first issued to troops on the Eastern Front in 1943 (2–32). The face shield at right incorporated a sight. The rocket projectile was inserted from behind.

U.S. armored columns and convoys moving through the Ardennes were constantly aware that the roads and surrounding terrain might well be infested with mines. The Tellermine 42 (2–33) was typical of the German mines the Allies encountered. It functioned when a pressure of one hundred pounds to five hundred pounds on the top-mounted pressure plate caused the hexagonal cap to operate a plunger/igniter assembly in the mine. A trip wire attached to the socket visible in front could also detonate the mine, as could an antilifting device attached to the bottom. Hence, the Americans referred to this weapon as the "triple threat mine."

Once their offensive got under way, the Germans anticipated that the American engineers would contest their movements by blowing bridges across the many streams lacing through the Ardennes. Engineering units accompa-

nying the *Panzer* spearheads were equipped with various types of bridging equipment. One of these was the Brückengerät K bridge (2–34), an assault bridge capable of spanning gaps of thirty-one feet to sixty-three feet and of carrying heavy vehicles and light tanks.

Though the Germans hoped that the Ardennes Offensive would be the first step in pushing the Allies back to the English Channel, preparations for defense in the event it failed were already in place. The Siegfried Line of obstacles and fortifications (2–35) provided the Germans with one last man-made barrier between the Fatherland and the advancing Allied armies.

The once-mighty *Luftwaffe* played only a limited support role in the Ardennes Offensive. The ten fighter groups made available to Operation *Bodenplatte* were composed primarily of the two aircraft types pictured in photo 2–36, although some late-model Messerschmitt Me-109K-4s were mixed in along with some long-nosed Focke-Wulf FW-190D-9s in JG-2 and JG-26. The Me-109's opened canopy shown here is of the newer so-called (by the Allies) Galland hood variety, which allowed for greater visibility to the sides and to the rear. Note from the position of the ailerons that the fighter's control stick has been pushed back to the left.

2-34. A German Brückengerät K small box-girder bridge captured near Stavelot, Belgium.

2-35. American troops prepare to blow up German "dragon's teeth" tank obstacles in the Siegfried Line.

2-36. *Luftwaffe* fighter aircraft are strewn about an abandoned German airfield at Bad Aibling, Germany. An Me-109G-14 sits in the foreground, while a *Schwarm* (flight) of four FW-190A-8s or A-9s is parked across the taxiway.

THE U.S. INFANTRY DIVISION

While somewhat similar in structure to the *Volksgrenadier* division, the U.S. infantry division's composition was clearly distinguishable from its German counterpart. Although both organizations were "triangulated" with three infantry regiments each, U.S. regiments had three full battalions, while the German regiments had only two thinly manned battalions.

Generally, four field artillery battalions were attached to each U.S. infantry division, including one battalion of heavy long-range guns (such as 155mm) and three battalions of 105mm howitzers. As an added guard against armored attack, one tank destroyer (TD) battalion of thirty-six vehicles was attached to most divisions, as were tank battalions in some units, such as the 1st Infantry Division. *Volksgrenadier* divisions tended to have far fewer such armored vehicles, having to rely on perhaps fourteen assault guns.

When reviewing German unit strengths and capabilities in the order of battle for the Ardennes, clearly the Germans placed the lion's share of their slender resources in the *Panzer* divisions. If the armored columns failed in the offensive, the worn-down, short-handed *Volksgrenadier* divisions would not be equipped to deal with the consequences. With greater depth and more internal resources for sustained fighting, the U.S. infantry division was to prove a far stronger and more versatile instrument of war.

EQUIPMENT OF THE AMERICAN FOOT SOLDIER

General Patton called the Garand M1 semiautomatic rifle (2–37) "the greatest battle implement ever devised." It was as much the symbol of the American infantryman as the MP-40 was of the German. The 9.5-pound weapon had a .30-caliber eight-round clip that could be fired by a trained marksman in about twenty seconds. Its disadvantages were that single rounds could not be loaded from the top and that, upon a soldier's firing his eighth round, the ejected clip clinking to the ground signaled an alert enemy that his foe's gun was not loaded.

That the Garand was certainly a precision weapon and that the average American infantryman was well trained to fire and hit a discrete target had at least the potential of working against American infantrymen in the Ardennes. Frequently in the chaos of close-quarters fighting, it was impossible to discern individual targets, which kept the Americans from firing. Conversely, because the Germans infused great numbers of area weapons (such as machine pistols) into their depleted *Volksgrenadier* companies, German soldiers were more likely to give any suspicious tree or patch of brush a good spraying.

The M1 carbine (2–38) was developed to provide driv-

2-37. Sgt. Ray McCrary of Ft. Smith, Arkansas—the first soldier of the 6th Armored Division to set foot on German soil—poses with his Garand M1 rifle for a Signal Corps photographer.

2-38. Tech/4 Fred Parke clutches his M1 carbine in an obviously posed action photo.

ers, machine gunners, mortar men, and other "non-shooting" personnel a more suitable weapon than a pistol. Long after the war, 1st Armored Division veteran John D. Conner summed up the M1 carbine's limitations: although the carbine was coveted for its light weight, its range was much inferior to that of the rifle. While the carbine was undoubtedly a handy, lightweight weapon, its shorter barrel (eighteen inches opposed to twenty-four inches for the rifle) and shorter, pistollike cartridge and bullet curtailed its effective range considerably. That characteristic could prove significant in the wide open spaces of North Africa or on an invasion beach, but the close proximity of the

2–39. Pvt. Edwin L. Larsen from the 3rd Armored Division cradles a Thompson M1 submachine gun.

2–40. Firing demonstration of the U.S. M3 submachine gun, or "grease gun."

combatants in the Ardennes tended to nullify this disadvantage. There, the carbine held its own.

Pictured in 2–39 is a soldier armed with a Thompson M1 submachine gun with a thirty-round box magazine. These simplified versions differed from the M1928 version in that they would not accept the large drum magazine so often associated with the gangster era of the 1920s and 1930s. Also, a simple, straight wooden grip replaced the front handle.

At the beginning of the war, the Thompson was the only submachine gun available to the army. Development proceeded on what became the M3 (2–40), a cheap substitute for the Thompson fabricated primarily from stamped parts. On Christmas Eve 1942, the army approved the M3 for production.

Weapons platoons made frequent use of both water-cooled and air-cooled versions of the Browning .30-caliber machine gun (2–41 and 2–42). Used against

2–41. A 5th Infantry Division crew sets up a Browning M1917A1 .30-caliber water-cooled machine gun.

2–42. Cpl. William Tamanatini of the 5th Armored Division loads a snow-covered Browning .30-caliber air-cooled machine gun near Sourbrodt, Belgium, on New Year's Day 1945.

2–43. Browning .50-caliber M2 machine gun mounted on a jeep.

personnel, lightly-armored vehicles, and even tanks, the .50-caliber machine gun (2–43) was devastatingly effective. It was also used as an antiaircraft weapon.

Based on a British design, the Mark 11A1 fragmentation grenade (2–44) first appeared during World War I. Its pattern remained standard throughout World War II and was phased out during the postwar period. When the war began, the Army did not have light antitank weapons. The M9 rifle-fired grenade resulted from efforts to fill this void. As photo 2–45 attests, however, Americans frequently employed the grenades in an antipersonnel role.

During the Ardennes Offensive, the Americans desperately needed winter camouflage clothing. After snow capes were made available, casualties dropped significantly in the snow-covered Ardennes (2–46).

The wet, cold weather forced the Americans to make certain field adaptations to their clothing. At Col. Banner P. Perdue's suggestion, a large quantity of captured German blankets were converted to woolen booties (2–47). These were worn while the soldiers' wet combat boots and socks dried out in front of a fire. When not wearing them, soldiers stuffed them into their shirts to keep their stomachs warm.

2–44. Mark 11A1 fragmentation grenades lie on the camouflaged hood of a jeep. Note the M3 submachine gun at right and its extra box magazine on the hood.

2-45. Three American soldiers—one (*left*) armed with an M1 carbine and two others with M1 rifles employed as launchers for M9 antitank grenades—gingerly approach the entrance to a building in Stavelot.

2-46. Two American soldiers demonstrate the camouflage value of the army's snow capes, which unfortunately were not generally available during the early stages of the Ardennes campaign.

2-47. Wool "booties," an innovation of Col. Banner P. Purdue, commanding officer of the 120th Infantry Regiment, 30th Infantry Division.

THE U.S. ARMORED DIVISION

Like its sister organizations in the other arms, the U.S. armored division changed considerably after the United States entered World War II. Put simply, by 1944 armored divisions were composed of matching sets of three battalions each of tanks, armored infantry, and artillery, accompanied by the usual assortment of engineering, reconnaissance, and signal units.

While the combined tank and infantry battalions were nominally designated regiments, their components, along with the artillery battalions, could be separated and recombined in any manner appropriate to the situation under two combat command headquarters (CCA and CCB) and a reserve headquarters (CCR). The army took certain liberties even with this loose organization, attaching additional infantry regiments and tank destroyer battalions.

In practice, the combat command idea was somewhat similar to the German *Kampfgruppe* (battle group) concept, which likewise recombined units into a mix best suited to meet the problem at hand. Such built-in flexibility lent itself admirably to the wildly fluid and chaotic conditions so often encountered on the battlefield.

U.S. TANKS, OTHER VEHICLES, AND WEAPONS

More than any other vehicle, the M4 Sherman tank (2–48) came to symbolize the U.S. armored legions that swept across Europe during 1944–45. The Sherman was the most important and widely used armored vehicle in service with the western Allied forces during World War II.

Early models mounted a 75mm M3 gun that was not nearly as powerful or effective as the *Wehrmacht*'s equivalent in the PzKpfw IVs and Panthers. The higher-velocity 76mm gun (actually a three-inch gun adapted for tank use) was installed on later-model Shermans, in particular the M4A3 (2–49). The gun was also threaded to receive an optional muzzle brake.

After D-Day, disillusionment set in even with the 76mm gun. General Bradley remarked that the gun "scuffed rather than penetrated" the armor of the German Panthers and Tigers. After Normandy, the tankers of the European theater of operations (ETO) asked that production of the 76mm guns be stopped in favor of the 90mm gun. Particularly in the wake of the Ardennes Offensive, tankers knew they needed a more powerful gun than the 76mm. Greater firepower was their prime universal concern, with speed and armor protection being secondary considerations.

The tank destroyer was developed in reaction to the German blitzkrieg in Europe. The Allies urgently needed to find a means to stop armored attacks and to prove the tank's vulnerability. Their answer seemed to lie in a vehicle that was more lightly armed and more maneuverable than a tank and that could rely on surprise and ambush for protection.

One of the results of this development was the M10 (2–50), which mounted a three-inch M7 gun. In compensation for its scant protection (which gave it more mobility than a tank), the sides of the vehicle and thinly armored open-top turret were sloped to deflect enemy gunfire. The M10 was typical of the 12th Army Group's tank destroyers. Although several tank destroyer battalions retained their M10s until the war's end, most units transitioned to the M36. One TD battalion of thirty-six vehicles was generally assigned to each infantry division.

2-48. Men of the 75th Division trudge behind an M4 Sherman tank near Basse, Belgium, on 10 January 1945 during the drive to relieve the 82d Airborne Division.

2-49. This M4A3 Sherman tank on highway H-4 near Bastogne mounts a 76mm gun, equipped in this case with a muzzle brake.

Rather than adapting an existing tank chassis, the M18 tank destroyer (2–51) was designed from scratch. It also differed from the M10 in that it had five sets of large road wheels. This characteristic, together with the muzzle brake on its 76mm M1A1 gun, frequently caused them to be identified (by Signal Corps photographers) as German Panthers! As the M18's armor ranged only from one-quarter inch to one inch, it was lighter than the M10 by twenty-five thousand pounds. On level ground, the M18 could reach the astonishing speed of 50 to 55 miles per hour, enabling it to scamper around the larger, more cumbersome German armor. M18-equipped units retained their vehicles throughout the war.

2-50. M10 Wolverine tank destroyer supports the drive of the 5th Division through Echternach, Luxembourg, in February 1945.

2-51. M18 Hellcat tank destroyer.

2-52. M36 tank destroyer at Dudelange, Luxembourg, 3 January 1945.

2-53. A U.S. M3 half-track of the 11th Armored Division prepares for an
attack on the outskirts of Bastogne, New Year's Eve, 1944.

The M36 tank destroyer (2–52) was a curiosity in that its development incorporated simultaneous forward and backward steps. Its increased firepower was due to a decision made in October 1942 to try to adapt the 90mm anti-aircraft gun to an antitank role. The vehicles's design was based on the M10 hull (in turn, based on the M4A3 chassis). Demand for this powerful new tank destroyer grew steadily in the months following D-Day, as the 90mm gun proved the best weapon in the U.S. arsenal to penetrate the heavy German armor. One of the greatest problems associated with tank destroyers was that, all too frequently, they were used as tanks, a role for which they were ill-suited on account of their thin armor.

The half-track (2–53) was "home" to the armored infantry soldier. His life centered around his vehicle, which provided motor transport and living space for a rifle squad.

Self-propelled guns (2–54) were frequently employed in the field artillery battalions attached to infantry divisions. These weapons were typically used to destroy prepared defensive positions. Photos 2–55 through 2–58 illustrate various types of guns the battalions used.

2-54. A U.S. 155mm self-propelled gun near Echternach.

2-55. American gun crewmen of the 770th Field Artillery Battalion dig an emplacement for their 4.5-inch gun near Wilwerdange, Luxembourg.

2-56. A 105mm howitzer gun crew from the 84th Division prepares to bombard enemy positions near La Roche, Belgium.

2-57. Two 90mm antiaircraft guns of the 214th Antiaircraft Artillery (AAA) Battalion point skyward. Such guns provided much of the heavy, long-range punch required to fend off any possible large-scale German attack from the skies.

2-58. A 40mm gun attached to the 633rd AAA Battalion, 80th Infantry Division, keeps watch over the town of Wiltz, Luxembourg. Note the white paint job applied, albeit hurriedly, to this intermediate-range mount.

2-59. Quadruple .50-caliber Browning machine-gun mount.

2-60. Parabolic radar antenna used by the 129th AAA Battalion near Differdange, Luxembourg.

The machine-gun mounts illustrated in 2–59 provided short-range antiaircraft support. They frequently appeared on M3 half-tracks. Note the kill marks registered on the shielding in front. Photos 2–60 through 2–62 show various aircraft-locater devices.

Heavy-weapons companies in U.S. infantry divisions were also equipped with mortars that were useful in clearing defensive positions. The 60mm mortar pictured in photo 2–63 was a scaled-down version of the 81mm

mortar. It could hurl a three-pound projectile nineteen hundred yards. The projectile's explosive force was comparable to a 75mm artillery shell. Mortars had several advantages: they could be taken into areas inaccessible to the larger artillery pieces, their firing positions were far easier to conceal, and their 100,000-candlepower star shells could also provide battlefield illumination. An experienced team could fire mortars at a rate of eighteen rounds per minute.

2-61. IFF (Identification, Friend or Foe) antenna set up by the 217th AAA Battalion sits in the snow near Bastogne.

2-62. An M7 aircraft locator device sits in a sandbagged position of the 217th AAA Battalion.

2–63. Two soldiers set up an M2 60mm mortar.

2–64. Test-firing of an M1 2.36-inch antitank rocket launcher, or bazooka.

As the army's standard light antitank weapon, the bazooka (2–64) could hurl a 3.4-pound rocket at three hundred feet per second into a target up to four hundred yards away. These characteristics compared quite favorably to the German Panzerfaust and Panzerschreck. The term *bazooka* came to be associated with this weapon via comedian Bob Burns, who called a complicated wind instrument he had invented the "bazooka." The similarity between his fierce-looking invention and the rocket launcher was too striking to miss, and the name stuck.

When the snow began to fall in December 1944, impromptu paint jobs such as illustrated in photo 2–65 became the order of the day. Those U.S. vehicles in olive-drab paint were all too easy to spot when silhouetted against the snowy backdrop of the Ardennes. The troops also used camouflage netting (2–66) to hide stationary equipment and vehicles.

Frequently, GI inventiveness met a particular challenge. The wretched road conditions encountered in the Ardennes once the columns moved off the paved thor-

2–65. Carl Listro of the 4th Armored Division applies a coat of white paint to a bulldozer of the 24th Armored Engineer Battalion in Luxembourg.

2–66. Pvt. Floyd Pilcheo of the 565th AAA Battalion adjusts camouflage netting on a two-and-a-half-ton truck.

oughfares spurred the inspiration of at least one clever American (2–67).

The opaque, gray skies of the Belgian winter severely handicapped American airpower during the Ardennes Offensive; however, once the clouds broke, German armored columns would be at the mercy of the U.S. fighter pilots. Employed as fighter-bombers, the P-47s (2–68) of Maj. Gen. Pete Quesada's IX Tactical Air Command would prove to be a decisive factor in the struggle of Hodges's First Army against Hitler's offensive.

The 422d and 425th Night Fighter squadrons of the IX and XIX Tactical Air commands provided yeoman service both before and during the German offensive. They sniffed out enemy armor and troop concentrations in the Ardennes, despite the fact that each squadron consisted of only several worn-out A-20s (2–69) and ten P-61s (2–70). The C-47s (2–71) of the IX Transport Command also kept the troops at Bastogne supplied during that bitter last week of December 1944.

2–67. Tech/4 Luther May of Colorado Springs, Colorado, proudly displays special "mud shoes" of his own invention that are installed on a jeep of the 981st Maintenance Battalion.

2–68. Republic P-47 Thunderbolts warm up on the tarmac somewhere in Normandy.

2–69. Douglas A-20 Havoc.

2-70. North American P-61 Black Widow.

2-71. Douglas C-47, the workhorse of the IX Transport Command.

CHAPTER 3

The Battle Plan, Objectives, and Orders of Battle

On 25 September 1944 Hitler, Wilhelm Keitel, and Alfred Jodl attended a meeting at Hitler's headquarters in East Prussia, during which the Führer laid out his assessment of Germany's current situation. He also directed Jodl to draft an operational plan for an offensive on the Western Front consistent with Hitler's assessment. Hitler had already been consulting with Jodl on this subject for about three weeks and now knew exactly what he wanted. So, in effect, he presented Jodl with the strategic plan and left Jodl to work out how it could be accomplished.

Hitler had selected as the point of attack a large sector extending from the Aachen area to the southern Luxembourg–France boundary. Here the U.S. First Army had stationed only one armored and four infantry divisions. To the north, Sepp Dietrich's 6. Panzer-Armee would set out from a position near Monschau, a pretty little town some twenty miles southeast of Aachen. Manteuffel's 5. Panzer-Armee would depart from the Schnee Eifel plateau near Prüm while Brandenburger's 7. Armee would launch itself from the south, not far from where the Moselle River touched the West Wall, or what the Allies called the Siegfried Line. The Sixth and Fifth armies would drive to Antwerp, with the Seventh and other units protecting the flank.

The loss of Antwerp to the British on 4 September had been a real blow for the Germans, because the Allies gained a prime port relatively close to the battle zone. True, the Scheldt Estuary had not been cleared, and, until it was, the Allies could not use the port facilities. In fact, Antwerp would not open to full Allied use until 26 November. But Hitler knew this was only a question of time. With the city back in German hands, the flow of British and American supplies and replacements would be seriously handicapped.

As of the 25 September meeting, Hitler planned to launch his offensive between 20 and 30 November and hoped to reach the Meuse River by the third day of the drive. He was sure the Allies could not react quickly enough to halt the offensive. "It will be another Dunkirk," he boasted.

He estimated the plan would require a minimum of thirty divisions, of which at least ten should be armored. Two circumstances were essential: speed and secrecy. The terrain would help with the latter, the woods offering concealment for the preparations. Also, the attack must come during weather that would ground the Allied air forces.

In the plan Hitler wanted Jodl to include estimates of the forces required and an order covering security and camouflage. Keitel would report on the amount of fuel and ammunition needed. And Rundstedt would be ordered to send certain *Panzer* units to Westphalia, ostensibly for "reorganization and training." As yet, Rundstedt was not included in the circle of those in the know.

On 9 October Jodl delivered to Hitler a plan that laid out five possible avenues of attack, with the northernmost springing from the area near Düsseldorf toward Antwerp and with one in the south driving toward Dijon. Each of these relatively modest ventures called for thirty-one divisions, a third of which were to be armored or armored infantry. Keitel estimated that between four million and five million gallons of fuel would be required, along with fifty trainloads of ammunition. Hitler instructed Jodl to enlarge the plan and combine the two northern-most attack routes.

The result was a plan code-named *Wacht am Rhein* (Watch on the Rhine) with the two-fold strategy of a drive on Antwerp and encircling the Allied armies west of the Meuse River. The force selected for the offensive was Generalfeldmarschall Walter Model's Heeresgruppe B, with Sepp Dietrich's 6. Panzer-Armee on the right, Manteuffel's 5. Panzer-Armee in the center, and Erich Brandenburger's 7. Armee pressing from the left (3–1).

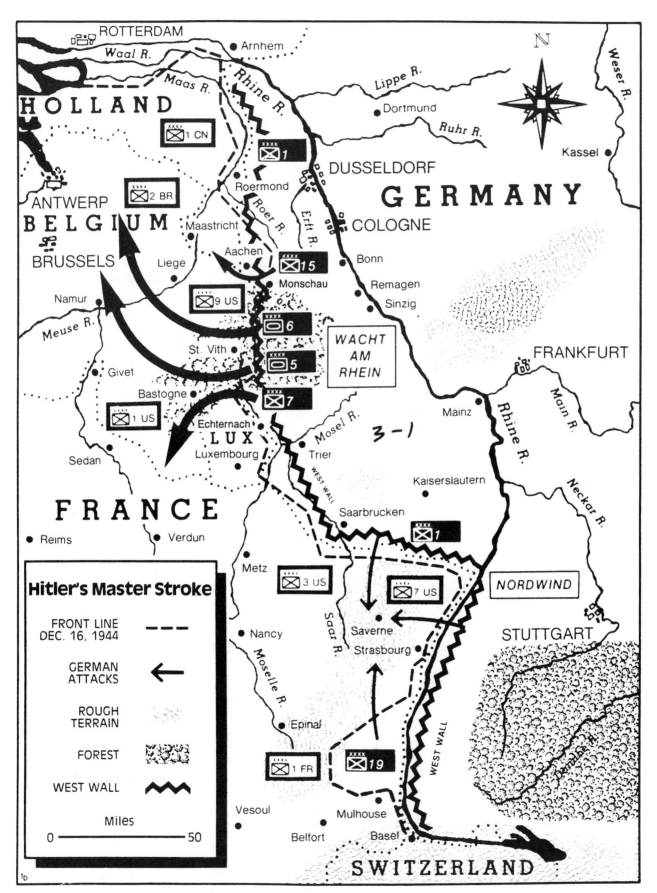

3-1. Final attack plan for the Ardennes Offensive showing the route of Model's Heeresgruppe B.

Of course, Hitler added a few grace notes to the score, summoning Obersturmbannführer Otto Skorzeny, the commando leader who had rescued Mussolini in 1943. Hitler promoted Skorzeny to lieutenant colonel and charged him with a behind-the-scenes mission. He was to form units of men wearing U.S. uniforms to cause confusion among the Americans and "give false orders and upset their communications, sending bodies of troops in the wrong direction." This would require recruiting men who spoke excellent English.

Not until 21 October were Rundstedt's and Model's chiefs of staff summoned to be briefed on *Wacht am Rhein* and report to their superiors. Model considered the plan "damn moldy" while Rundstedt thought it had "a touch of genius" but was unrealistic. Rundstedt worked up an alternate plan whereby the German's main thrust would meet near Liège and there envelop the Allied forces preparing to attack the Ruhr. Meanwhile, Model tried hard to convince Hitler that the Germans did not have the means to reach Antwerp. Predictably, both men failed to budge the Führer, who even added a second attack to be launched when the Allies reacted against the *Panzer* divisions. Rundstedt, Model, and Manteuffel, however, were so sure capturing Antwerp was unrealistic that they made no plans extending beyond the Meuse.

Rundstedt's analysis seems a fair summation. The plan had scope and daring and looked fine on paper. The Germans had struck through the Ardennes in 1940; had conquered Luxembourg, Belgium, Holland, and France, and had driven the British back to their native islands. In the context of late 1944, however, the concept was unrealistic. This was perhaps inevitable, because Hitler had become increasingly divorced from reality. He suffered from the occupational disease of dictators—isolation. He seldom left his East Prussia headquarters, and was more and more dependent upon maps and charts rather than firsthand or even secondhand knowledge. Since the attempt on his life in July 1944, he tended to regard any word of pessimism or caution as evidence of disloyalty or lack of patriotism. Naturally, his subordinates hesitated to bring him bad news.

A prime example of Hitler's unrealistic expectations is his rationale behind *Wacht am Rhein*. He was convinced that the Grand Alliance was unnatural and fragile, and would disintegrate in the face of a major German victory. He is even said to have remarked that the British might join him in driving the Americans out of Europe. That could have been his idea of a joke; nevertheless, he did have a certain respect for the British and a low opinion of Americans. Obsessed with his concept of a "pure" race, he could not conceive that Americans, with their varied backgrounds, could truly be courageous, reliable soldiers.

How much Hitler actually knew about the divisions in the Allied ranks is questionable, but of course many and serious differences of opinion existed and were thoroughly aired. What Hitler seems not to have understood is that these arguments were over means, not ends. On their objective—defeat of Germany—there was no question.

Hitler was equally irrational in his assessment of Germany's ability to mount and carry through an offensive of this magnitude. Almost without air support, he was initiating a major move with reconstituted divisions, inadequate fuel and supplies into an area whose road system could barely support tanks—all in the dead of winter. He had going for him initial surprise, short supply lines, some intelligent generals, and brave men. They proved to be not enough.

GERMAN ORDER OF BATTLE

Here then are the units and their commanders charged with translating Hitler's grandiose pipe dream into a workable military operation. The 6. SS-Panzer-Armee consisted of the units in figure 3–2.

3–2: ORGANIZATION OF THE 6. PANZER-ARMEE

6. Panzer-Armee	Oberstgruppenführer Josef Dietrich
I. SS-Panzerkorps	Gruppenführer Hermann Priess
1. SS-Panzer-Div.	Oberführer Wilhelm Mohnke
12. SS-Panzer-Div.	Standartenführer Hugo Kraas
12. Volksgrenadier-Div.	Generalmajor Gerhardt Engel
277. Volksgrenadier-Div.	Oberst Wilhelm Viebig
3. Fallschirmjager-Div.	Generalmajor Walter Wadehn
II. SS-Panzerkorps	Obergruppenführer Willi Bittrich
2. SS-Panzer-Div.	Bridgadeführer Heinz Lammerding
9. SS-Panzer-Div.	Oberführer Sylvester Stadler
LXVII. Armeekorps (attached)	Generalleutnant Otto Hitzfeld
272. Volksgrenadier-Div.	Oberst Georg Kosmalla
326. Volksgrenadier-Div.	Oberst Erwin Kaschner

3–3. SS-Oberführer Wilhelm Mohnke (left), 1. SS-Panzer-Division _Leibstandarte Adolf Hitler_, shown here greeting Sepp Dietrich.

3–4. SS-Standartenführer Hugo Kraas, 12. SS-Panzer-Division _Hitlerjugend_, shown here as an Obersturmbannführer.

On 20 August 1944, Oberführer Wilhelm Mohnke (3–3) took command of the veteran 1. SS-Panzer-Division, _Leibstandarte Adolf Hitler_. As a regiment, and later as a division, this unit fought from the invasion of Poland through the titanic struggles on the Eastern Front, and the Allies' drive through France. The division narrowly escaped from the Falaise pocket,* breaking out with only thirty tanks. Early in November, it withdrew east of the Rhine for rehabilitation near Sieburg in Westphalia. When the Ardennes Offensive opened, the division was up to 90 percent strength in men (with many conscripts) and 80 percent in tanks. The 1. SS-Panzer-Division was to spearhead the thrust into the American positions in the Ardennes and, together with the 12. SS-Panzer-Division _Hitlerjugend_ (Hitler Youth), drive for the Meuse and establish bridgeheads there. Then alongside the II. SS-Panzerkorps, it would race for Antwerp.

After the Americans captured the 12. SS-Panzer-Division _Hitlerjugend_'s famed commander, Oberführer Kurt "Panzer" Meyer, in September, Standartenführer Hugo Kraas (3–4) assumed command in November 1944, holding that post through the end of the war. The division was relatively new, having been formed as a _Panzergrenadier_ division in June 1943. As its name implied, the division recruited directly from the ranks of the Hitler Youth. A large percentage of the officer leadership came from the 1. SS-Panzer-Division. _Hitlerjugend_ commenced training as a division in January 1944, seeing its first action in the savage fighting near Caen during the Normandy campaign. Trapped in the Falaise pocket, remnants of the division escaped with only six hundred men and no tanks.

After rebuilding to a level comparable to the _Leibstandarte,_ the division was committed to the Ardennes Offensive, with the task of operating on the right flank of the 1. SS-Panzer-Division and assaulting Elsenborn Ridge.

Two infantry divisions assigned to the I. SS-Panzerkorps shouldered the burden of making the initial breakthroughs for the _Panzer_ divisions behind to exploit. The 12. Volksgrenadier-Division under Generalmajor Gerhardt Engel (3–5) was experienced, relatively intact, and Dietrich's best infantry division. The 277. Volksgrenadier-Division had been mauled in Normandy and withdrew to

3–5. Generalmajor Gerhardt Engel, 12. Volksgrenadier-Division, shown earlier in his career as a Hauptmann.

*Characteristically, Hitler had ordered Falaise held to the last man, but the Canadians and Americans so narrowed the escape route that the Germans fled in disorganized panic.

3–6. Oberst Georg Kosmalla, 272. Volksgrenadier-Division, had formerly led the 32. Infanterie-Division on the northern sector of the Russian Front.

3–7. SS-Brigadeführer Heinz Lammerding, 2. SS-Panzer-Division *Das Reich,* as a Standartenführer.

Hungary for rebuilding before being sent back west to the Ardennes under Oberst Wilhelm Viebig (not pictured).

The 3. Fallschirmjäger-Division, which accompanied the SS spearheads, trained as a parachute division but fought out the war as an infantry division. It had been ground to pieces in the Falaise and Mons pockets, and its replacements were largely inexperienced *Luftwaffe* ground and aircrew personnel.

Generalleutnant Otto Hitzfeld's LXVII. Armeekorps (borrowed from the 15. Armee) was to break out along the northern edge of Elsenborn Ridge and form a defensive line with Dietrich's other infantry divisions to meet any American reaction to the initial assaults. Following the hoped-for breach of the Meuse, Hitzfeld's command would revert to the 15. Armee. Both of his divisions, the 272., under Oberst Georg Kosmalla (3–6), and 326. Volksgrenadier, had been crushed in Normandy, rebuilt with inexperienced troops, and hastily redeployed in the West.

Bittrich's II. SS-Panzerkorps, composed of the 2. and 9. SS-Panzer-Divisions, respectively under Brigadeführer Heinz Lammerding (3–7) and Oberführer Sylvester Stadler (3–8), was to serve as the second wave behind the I. SS-Panzerkorps. Once Bittrich's divisions crossed the Meuse and were resupplied, both SS-Panzerkorps would proceed side by side to Antwerp.

The units in figure 3–9 comprised the 5. Panzer-Armee, located to the left of the 6. Panzer-Armee.

3–8. SS-Oberführer Sylvester Stadler, 9. SS-Panzer-Division *Hohenstaufen,* shown here as an Obersturmbannführer.

3–9: ORGANIZATION OF THE 5. PANZER-ARMEE

5. Panzer-Armee	General d. Pz. Tr. Hasso v. Manteuffel
LXVI. Armeekorps	General d. Art. Walter Lucht
18. Volksgrenadier-Div.	Oberst Günther Hoffmann-Schönborn
62. Volksgrenadier-Div.	Oberst Frederich Kittel
LVIII. Panzerkorps	General d. Pz. Tr. Walter Krüger
116. Panzer-Div.	Generalmajor Siegfried v. Waldenburg
560. Volksgrenadier-Div.	Oberst Rudolf Langenhaeuser
XLVII. Panzerkorps	General d. Pz. Tr. Heinrich v. Lüttwitz
2. Panzer-Div.	Oberst Meinrad v. Lauchert
Panzer-Lehr-Div.	Generalleutnant Fritz Bayerlein
26. Volksgrenadier-Div.	Oberst Heinz Kokott

Manteuffel's 5. Panzer-Armee would advance toward the Meuse to the left of the 6. Panzer-Armee, with Lucht's LXVI. Korps on Dietrich's flank, while the LVIII. and XLVII. Panzerkorps advanced in the center and left respectively. After securing bridgeheads over the Meuse, Manteuffel would attack toward Antwerp, at the same time providing protection for Dietrich's left.

Formed in September 1944, the 18. Volksgrenadier was commanded by Oberst Günther Hoffmann-Schönborn (3–10). It had absorbed much of a *Luftwaffe* field division, plus large numbers of naval personnel and leftovers from the hastily organized 571. Grenadier-Division. Despite its motley makeup, the division fought well.

Having suffered heavy casualties throughout the war in the East, Oberst Frederich Kittel's (3–11) 62. Volksgrenadier-Division was withdrawn for rebuilding in September 1944. The U.S. 9th Infantry Division would destroy it in the battles near Monschau.

Through its progenitor units, Generalmajor Siegfried von Waldenburg's (3–12) 116. Panzer, nicknamed the "Greyhound Division," had a long, distinguished record

3-10. Oberst Günther Hoffmann-Schönborn, 18. Volksgrenadier-Division.

3-12. Generalmajor Siegfried von Waldenburg, 116. Panzer-Division.

3-11. Oberst Frederich Kittel (here a Generalmajor), 62. Volksgrenadier-Division.

3-13. Oberst Meinrad von Lauchert, 2. Panzer-Division.

3-14. Generalleutnant Fritz Bayerlein, *Panzer-Lehr*-Division, shown here in March 1944 during Operation *Margarethe* in Hungary.

of service. Originally the 16. Infanterie-Division, it was motorized in September 1940 and fought in the Balkans and Ukraine in 1941 as the 16. Panzergrenadier-Division. The unit suffered heavy losses in Russia during 1943 and withdrew to France where it was reconstituted as the 116. Panzer-Division in March 1944. Committed against the western Allies in the Normandy campaign, the 116. Panzer-Division was among the German units encircled at Falaise, breaking out with heavy losses. Like so many other divisions, it was again rebuilt during September and October 1944, just in time for the Ardennes Offensive.

Formed in 1935, the 2. Panzer-Division, now under Oberst Meinrad von Lauchert (3–13), had rendered distinguished service to the Fatherland from the campaigns in Poland and France to the gates of Moscow. It was typical of the units that had fought for the entire war on both fronts. After suffering heavy losses in 1943, it was withdrawn and rebuilt, only to be chewed up in the Falaise pocket and rebuilt yet again prior to the Ardennes campaign.

Panzer-Lehr-Division, commanded by Generalleutnant Fritz Bayerlein (3–14), was formed in January 1944 from various armored demonstration units and training schools, and was considered a crack outfit from the start. Although it served during the occupation of Hungary early in 1944, the division's first real test came during the Normandy campaign, where it proved to be one of the hardest-fighting divisions in the German army. Prior to the Ardennes Offensive, *Panzer-Lehr* was fighting the Americans as late as November along the Saar River. A

quick refit brought the unit back to about 80 percent strength.

Originally the 26. Infanterie-Division, the sturdy 26. Volksgrenadier-Division had been only lightly engaged during the campaign in France. Then it had served primarily on the Eastern Front. The war in Russia found the 26. Infanterie continuously engaged from the initial penetration into the Soviet Union in 1941 to the bitter fighting during the battle of Kursk. Rebuilt as the 26. Volksgrenadier under Oberst Heinz Kokott (3–15), the division received large numbers of *Luftwaffe* and *Kriegsmarine*

3-15. Oberst Heinz Kokott, 26. Volksgrenadier-Division, as commanding officer of the Grenadier-Regiment 377.

3–16: ORGANIZATION OF THE 7. ARMEE

7. Armee	General d. Pz. Tr. Erich Brandenburger
LXXXV. Armeekorps	General d. Inf. Baptist Kniess
5. Fallschirmjäger-Div.	Oberst Ludwig Heilmann
352. Volksgrenadier-Div.	Oberst Erich Schmidt
LXXX. Armeekorps	General d. Inf. Franz Beyer
276. Volksgrenadier-Div.	Generalmajor Kurt Moehring
212. Volksgrenadier-Div.	Generalleutnant Franz Sensfuss
LIII. Armeekorps	General d. Kav. Edwin v. Rothkirch
Festungs-Infanterie-Battaillon 999	
Festungs-MG-Battaillon 44	

personnel who, despite their varied backgrounds, mixed well with the veteran cadres to form one of the best of the *Volksgrenadier* divisions.

Brandenburger's 7. Armee, on the left flank of the offensive, was made up of the units in 3–16.

The mission of Brandenburger's divisions was to protect the left flank of the offensive by pressing forward north of Echternach and across the Saar within the limitations of their talent and strength. The Germans entertained no great expectations from the southern flank. Led by Erich Brandenburger, Model's least favorite commander, the 7. Armee was by far the weakest of the three armies. For the most part, the divisions comprising the 7. Armee were among those battered beyond recognition at Normandy, then filled with inexperienced and poorly led replacements gleaned from the navy, the air force, and from hospitals in the rear.

The 7. Armee presented a marked contrast to most of the *Waffen-SS* units and provided the crowning illustration of how Germany had nearly scratched through the bottom of the manpower barrel. The 7. Armee likewise was illustrated of the ill effects on efficiency and morale of concentrating the few good replacements into a minority of crack outfits. The fact that fortress defense troops and personnel from a disciplinary unit made up the primary strength of LIII. Armeekorps troops speaks for itself.

Typical of the problems faced by Brandenburger's division commanders were those of Generalmajor Ludwig Heilmann (3–17), commanding the 5. Fallschirmjäger-Division. He found that his division little resembled the efficient outfit of its pre-Normandy days. Heilmann's *Luftwaffe* ground troop replacements exhibited poor morale and worse unit cohesion.

Oberst Erich Schmidt (3–18) had his own problems with the 352. Volksgrenadier-Division. Although displaying some degree of morale and fighting spirit, this division's replacements from the navy had little experience in ground operations.

3–17. Oberst Ludwig Heilmann, 5. Fallschirmjäger-Division.

3–18. Oberst Erich Schmidt, 352. Volksgrenadier-Division.

3-19. Generalmajor Kurt Moehring, 276. Volksgrenadier-Division.

3-20. Generalleutnant Franz Sensfuss, 212. Volksgrenadier-Division.

Drawing heavily from German military hospitals, Generalmajor Kurt Moehring's (3–19) 276. Volksgrenadier-Division was a caricature of the infantry division that had been destroyed in Normandy and then reconstituted. It was sadly lacking in leadership and the will to continue the fight.

Brandenburger's one bright spot was the 212. Volksgrenadier, his best division. The eve of the offensive found it nearly up to full strength and led by efficient, experienced officers such as its commander, Generalleutnant Franz Sensfuss (3–20).

Like most large formations, Heeresgruppe B had access in an emergency to reserves established at various levels. These included the units in figure 3–21.

Five units, three armored and two infantry, from the OKW Reserves were allocated to the Ardennes Offensive. The *Führer-Begleit*-Brigade originated in 1939 as a motorized escort battalion for Hitler. Although the unit's station was at his headquarters in East Prussia, portions of the unit were sent into action on the Eastern Front. Meanwhile, *Führer-Begleit* was progressively upgraded to regiment and then to brigade status in November 1944 under Oberst Otto Remer (3–22).

Like the *Führer-Begleit*-Brigade, the *Führer-Grena-*

3–21: ORGANIZATION OF THE GERMAN RESERVES

OKW Reserves

Führer-Begleit-Brig.	Oberst Otto Remer
Führer-Grenadier-Brig.	Oberst Hans-Joachim Kahler
3. Panzer-grenadier-Div.	Generalmajor Walter Denkert
9. Volksgrenadier-Div.	Oberst Werner Kolb
167. Volksgrenadier-Div.	Generalleutnant Hans-Kurt Höcker

Heeresgruppe B Reserves

79. Volksgrenadier-Div.	Oberst Alois Weber

Reserves from 15. Armee

15. Panzergrenadier-Div.	Oberst Han-Joachim Deckert
9. Panzer-Div.	Generalmajor Harald v. Elverfeld
340. Volksgrenadier-Div.	Oberst Theodor Tolsdorff
246. Volksgrenadier-Div.	Oberst Peter Körte

3-22. Oberst Otto Remer,
   ***Führer-Begleit*-Brigade.**

3-23. Oberst Hans-Joachim Kahler,
   ***Führer-Grenadier*-Brigade.**

dier-Brigade, under Oberst Hans-Joachim Kahler (3–23) was an armored formation built around a single *Panzer* regiment with supporting artillery and assault gun battalions. First as its sister unit, *Führer-Grenadier* had gained considerable fighting experience on the Eastern Front.

The 9. Volksgrenadier-Division was nearly destroyed in August 1944 during the retreat in Romania. Under Oberst Werner Kolb (3–24), the division underwent rebuilding in Denmark late in the year in time for the Ardennes. By that time, however, most of the fighting spirit had been ground out of this once-proud division.

Generalleutnant Hans-Kurt Höcker (3–25) commanded the 167. A typical *Volksgrenadier* division, it was the predictable product of incorporating remnants of a *Luftwaffe* field division.

3-24. Oberst Werner Kolb,
   9. Volksgrenadier-Division.

3-25. Generalleutnant Hans-Kurt Höcker,
   167. Volksgrenadier-Division.

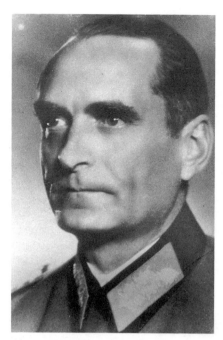

**3–26. Generalmajor Harald von Elverfeld,
9. Panzer-Division.**

**3–27. Oberst Theodor Tolsdorff,
340. Volksgrenadier-Division.**

The 15. Armee made four divisions available to *Wacht am Rhein.* The 9. Panzer under Generalmajor Harald von Elverfeld (3–26) was one of the stronger in terms of tanks and equipment and, like the 15. Panzergrenadier-Division, counted seventy-five tanks, assault guns, and tank destroyers in its inventory.

Committed to the battle in late December when it was attached to the I. SS-Panzerkorps, Oberst Theodor Tolsdorff's (3–27) 340. Volksgrenadier-Division had more veterans than most units of its type. Having come from the recent fighting near Aachen, however, it was badly understrength.

The 246. Volksgrenadier-Division, commanded by Oberst Peter Körte (3–28), had been another Eastern Front division destroyed and rebuilt with *Kriegsmarine* personnel around a small cadre of veterans and then sent into action in the West. The battlegrounds around Aachen were soaked with the blood of this division, twice rebuilt and destroyed. After a final infusion of *Luftwaffe* personnel, it was belatedly committed to the Battle of the Bulge in January 1945.

**3–28. Oberst Peter Körte, 246.
Volksgrenadier-Division.**

INITIAL U.S. DEPLOYMENT

Maj. Gen. Walter E. Lauer's (3–29) 99th Infantry Division was the primary target of the I. SS-Panzerkorps. Fresh from England with little experience, the 99th landed at Le Havre, France, on 3 November. The division first went into action on 13 December, attacking the Roer and Urft dams, and met heavy resistance. By 16 December, the division was spread thinly from Monschau to Losheim. Ironically, that sector had been considered a quiet one in which the fledgling division might gain some valuable experience before being committed to full-scale

3-29. Maj. Gen. Walter E. Lauer (*right center*), commanding general, 99th Infantry Division, presents the Presidential Unit Citation to the 3d Battalion, 195th Infantry Regiment, for its heroic defense during the German breakthrough in the Ardennes.

offensive operations. Later, Lauer's men suffered the ignominy of being among the American prisoners of war
photographed most often by the Germans during the offensive.

Maj. Gen. Walter M. Robertson's (3–30) 2d Infantry
Division, in action since the Normandy invasion, shared
with Lauer's 99th the burden of blunting the thrusts of
Dietrich's 6. Panzer-Armee. The 2d landed on Omaha
Beach on 7 June, and was heavily engaged during the entire summer, taking part in the drives against Saint-Lô and
Brest. In late September, the division moved by rail to the
Ardennes, and took up its position at St. Vith. Placed in
motion once again on 11 December for the campaigns
against the Roer and Urft dams, the division was diverted
to the Monschau Forest on 16 December to halt the German drive.

Further north, the 9th Infantry Division under Maj.
Gen Louis A. Craig was in a position to parry the blows
administered by Oberst Kosmalla's 272. Volksgrenadier-
Division. The 9th was one of the U.S. Army's workhorse
outfits, landing in North Africa on 8 November 1942, taking part in the Sicily campaign in the summer of 1943, and
later splashing ashore in France on 10 June 1944. It participated in the storming of Cherbourg, the drive on Saint-
Lô, and the reduction of the Falaise pocket. Autumn found

3-30. Maj. Gen. Walter M. Robertson, commanding general, 2d Infantry Division, pins the Legion of Merit on Lt. Col. Donald P. Christensen, 2d Infantry intelligence officer. Robertson's longevity was matched by few division commanders, for he led the 2d Infantry from May 1942 through the end of the war.

3–31. Maj. Gen. Norman S. Cota, commanding general, 28th Infantry Division, chats with General Eisenhower on 9 November 1944.

3–32. Maj. Gen. Raymond O. Barton, commanding general, 4th Infantry Division.

the 9th engaged once again, this time in the bitter fighting of the Huertgen Forest. During the initial German push into the Ardennes, the division would relieve the 2d and 99th divisions and defend the area near Monschau.

The 28th Infantry Division, composed initially of men from the Pennsylvania National Guard and led by Maj. Gen. Norman Cota (3–31), came ashore in Normandy during July 1944. It participated in the Saint-Lô campaign, and later in attacks against the West Wall and the Huertgen Forest. With the 106th Infantry Division, commanded by Maj. Gen. Alan W. Jones, the 28th faced the bulk of Manteuffel's 5. Panzer-Armee.

The 106th was one of the greenest American divisions in the Ardennes. Arriving in France on 6 December, it had little time to prove itself. After relieving the 2d Infantry Division in the Schnee Eifel sector, the 106th was struck hard when the German offensive commenced, losing 6,500 men as prisoners of war. Two entire infantry regiments, the 422d and 423d, were surrounded in the Eifel and surrendered, while the 424th was pushed across the Our River, losing practically all of its equipment in the process.

The 4th Infantry, or "Ivy," Division, commanded by Maj. Gen. Raymond O. Barton (3–32) was another veteran outfit from the campaigning in Normandy and northern France. With French units, it entered Paris and then drove quickly across France to participate in the West Wall assaults on the Schnee Eifel in September 1944 and the attacks in the Huertgen Forest. Relieved by the 83d Division, the 4th repaired to Luxembourg. Together with the 9th Armored Division under Maj. Gen. John W. Leonard, the 4th was in position to provide initial opposition

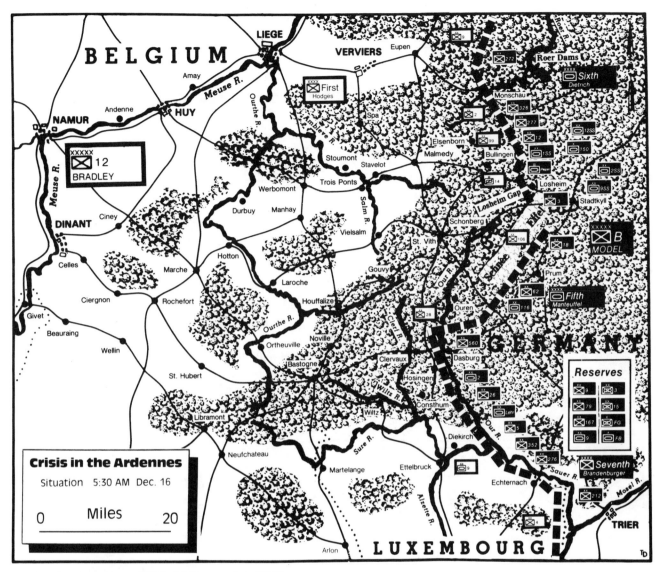

3-33. The Ardennes, 0530, 16 December 1944.

against Brandenburger's 7. Armee. Both divisions lay deployed west of the Saar near Echternach.

One of the more inexperienced U.S. armored formations in the Ardennes, the 9th Armored Division landed in France on 3 October. It spent the next two months patrolling the quiet sector adjacent to the German-Luxembourg border.

The map shown here (3–33) covers *Wacht am Rhein* as of 16 December. Within a week, matters had deteriorated to the point where Hitler was preparing a subsidiary plan to go into effect on New Year's Eve. Code-named *Nordwind* (North Wind), it called for a strike into Alsace with the object of forcing the Americans to pull back their divisions near the German southern flank of the *Wacht am Rhein* operation. The Ardennes Offensive could there upon proceed with renewed vigor.

This was not a bad idea, because the U.S. 6th Army Group and the First French Army were already overex-

tended on a line 240 miles long. This line included a bulge called the Colmar Pocket that worried Eisenhower no end. When five infantry and two armored divisions of the German 1. Armee attacked late on New Year's Eve, Eisenhower ordered Lt. Gen. Jacob L. Devers, the group commander, to retire to the Vosges and leave only a token screening force behind.

This order would necessitate abandoning Strasbourg, which precipitated a passionate but brief fight with de Gaulle and generals Pierre Juin and Jean de Lattre de Tassigny. Strasbourg had intense historical and cultural meaning to the French, who absolutely refused to let it go again. Fortunately, Ike had second thoughts and permitted the French to defend the city. In any case, *Nordwind* was a failure, and by 25 January 1945, when Hitler called it off, it had cost him 25,000 casualties and had had no effect upon the action in the Ardennes.

CHAPTER 4

The German Offensive Opens

THE ROLLBAHNEN AND I. SS.-PANZERKORPS

Although Dietrich's *Panzer* spearheads had been cast in the starring role in the upcoming offensive, the area designated for the I. SS-Panzerkorps (4–1) was entirely unsuitable for rapid movement, particularly by the heavier

German armor. A series of five *Rollbahnen,* or highways (literally "runways"), were selected for the 12. and 1. SS-Panzer divisions: *Rollbahnen* A, B, and C for *Hitlerjugend* and *Rollbahnen* D and E for the *Leibstandarte Adolf Hitler,* respectively.

The image of a runway—that is, wide and well paved—bore little resemblance to the thoroughfares reserved for SS-Gruppenführer Priess's two armored divi-

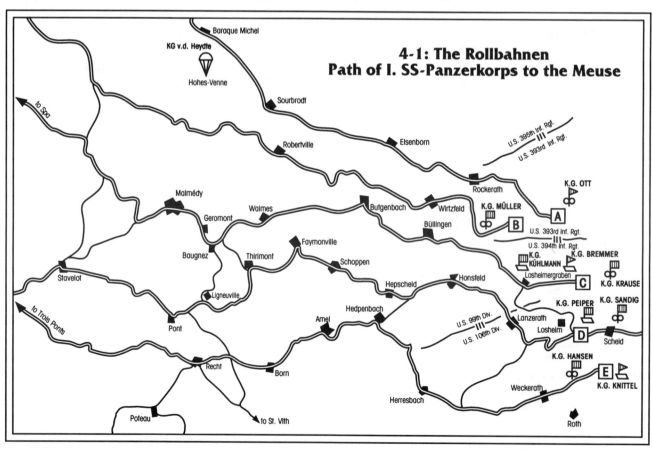

4-1: The Rollbahnen
Path of I. SS-Panzerkorps to the Meuse

The German Offensive Opens **53**

4–2. Sturmbannführer Siegfried Müller, SS-Panzergrenadier-Regiment 25.

4–3. Sturmbannführer Herbert Kühlmann, SS-Panzer-Regiment 12, while serving earlier in the war with the 1. SS-Panzer-Division.

sions. Although some were indeed paved, many miles consisted only of earthen trails through the woods whose soft surfaces promised to mire anything without tracks, and some with, in the event of a thaw.

Rollbahn A was set aside for *Hitlerjugend's* I/SS-Panzergrenadier-Regiment 25, which was commanded by Hauptsturmführer Alfons Ott. Accompanying Ott's battalion were two attached companies of engineers and artillery towed by prime movers. Their mission was to make contact with the paratroopers of Operation *Stösser* (Hawk) who were to land behind enemy lines and secure the main roads leading to the Meuse River.

Slated for *Rollbahn* B, *Kampfgruppe* Müller was composed of Sturmbannführer Siegfried Müller's (4–2) own SS-Panzergrenadier-Regiment 25 (less Ott's battalion)

and SS-Panzerjäger-Abteilung (tank destroyer battalion) 12 under Hauptsturmführer Karl-Hans Brockschmidt.

Three battle groups lay ready to charge forward on *Rollbahn* C, the last of the highways reserved for the 12. SS-Panzer-Division. In first position at the starting gate was *Kampfgruppe* Kühlmann, under Sturmbannführer Hubert Kühlman (4–3), with SS-Panzer-Regiment 12, schwere SS-Panzer-Abteilung 560, and III/SS-Panzergrenadier-Regiment 26, led by Hauptsturmführer Georg Urabl. In second position was Sturmbannführer Gerhard Bremer's (4–4) *Kampfgruppe*, composed of the *Hitlerjugend* division's reconnaissance battalion. The balance of Sturmbannführer Bernard Krause's (4–5) SS-Panzergrenadier-Regiment 26 brought up the rear in third position.

4–4. Sturmbannführer Gerhard Bremer, SS-Aufklärungs-Abteilung 12, while serving as an Obersturmführer with the 1. SS-Panzer-Division.

4–5. Sturmbannführer Bernhard Krause, SS-Panzergrenadier-Regiment 26.

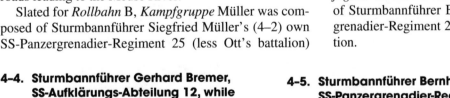

Rollbahn D was set aside for the use of *Kampfgruppe* Peiper, including Obersturmbannführer Joachim Peiper's (4–6) own SS-Panzer-Regiment 1, the third battalion from SS-Panzergrenadier-Regiment 2, and schwere SS-Panzer-Abteilung 501 under Obersturmbannführer Heinz von Westernhagen (4–7). Behind Peiper was *Kampfgruppe* Sandig, under Sturmbannführer Rudolf Sandig (4–8), with SS-Panzergrenadier-Regiment 2 and the staffs of Oberführer Mohnke and Gruppenführer Priess.

Accompanied by the division's tank destroyer battalion, Sturmbannführer Max Hansen's (4–9) battle group led the way on *Rollbahn* E with SS-Panzergrenadier-Regiment 1. Bringing up the rear on *Rollbahn* E was Sturmbannführer Gustav Knittel (4–10) with his SS-Panzer-Aufklärungs-Abteilung 1.

4–6. Obersturmbannführer Joachim Peiper, SS-Panzer-Regiment 1, as a Sturmbannführer. This photo is from a color portrait taken by official photographer Walter Frentz during Peiper's visit to the Führer's headquarters at Wolf's Lair. The original color print shows dark circles under Peiper's eyes, evidence of either fatigue and stress suffered on the Russian Front or perhaps a vitamin-C deficiency.

4–7. Dressed in a camouflage tunic, Obersturmbannführer Heinz von Westernhagen, schwere SS-Panzer-Abteilung 501, briefs officers (likely his company commanders) during the Normandy campaign.

4–8. Sturmbannführer Rudolf Sandig, SS-Panzergrenadier-Regiment 2.

4–9. Sturmbannführer Max Hansen, SS-Panzergrenadier-Regiment 1.

4–10. Sturmbannführer Gustav Knittel, SS-Panzer-Aufklärungs-Abteilung 1.

"WE MARCH!": CAPTURED GERMAN FILM OF THE OFFENSIVE

Compared to the multitudes of photographs available from the American perspective, relatively few German photographs detailing the Ardennes Offensive have survived and for several reasons. A substantial portion of the pictorial record that remained with the German armies was lost or destroyed in the campaign's aftermath. Moreover, in the days preceding their final defeat in May 1945, the Germans destroyed at least part of their military photographic archives. In addition, the widespread destruction of government offices and the confusion that prevailed during the last days of the war were hardly conducive to preserving records.

A most important glimpse into the Ardennes Offensive from the German vantage point does exist, however, in the form of four captured rolls of 35mm film. They were probably exposed by two or more *SS-Kriegsberichter,* or war correspondents, who accompanied elements of the 1. SS-Panzer-Division *Leibstandarte Adolf Hitler* and the 18. Volksgrenadier-Division. The only known details of the film's capture are that the U.S. 3d Armored Division seized the exposed film, along with a quantity of motion picture footage, and turned it over to the U.S. Signal Corps, which then duplicated most of the individual 35mm frames.

Although the location of the original film is unknown (it was likely discarded after copying), the processors of the German film fortunately recorded the original frame numbers and identified them according to their original rolls. Unfortunately, however, the prints are now spread out over a very wide range of negative numbers within the Signal Corps's collection in the U.S. National Archives. With many of the file contact prints missing or misfiled, only three-quarters of the prints have been located. Poorly exposed or out-of-focus frames might well account for those still missing.

Now preserved in the National Archives, these photographs allow us to view the German offensive through a unique window in time—to see the Germans as they saw themselves and what the *Kriegsberichter* wanted to preserve for posterity. Here, for the first time, the photographs exist together as a block in their original order.

Roll 1—16 or 17 December: The Advance Toward Büllingen; 1. SS-Panzer-Division—In the Wake of *Kampfgruppe* Peiper; 18. Volksgrenadier-Division; Hallschlag, Merlscheid, Losheimergraben, Roth, and Honsfeld

The American POWs from the 99th Infantry shown in photo 4–11 and those in other photographs of this series may have been captured at Honsfeld on 17 December. If so, they were lucky to be alive, because the victorious

4-11. Hallschlag, Germany. Cold hands in their pockets, prisoners from the U.S. 99th Infantry Division await marching instructions from a *Feldgendarm* (military policeman) at far right. Note the *Feldgendarmerie* gorget hanging around his neck.

4-12. The column in motion, American prisoners pass the *Kriegsberichter*. Two soldiers at left help guide a man with a facial wound.

4-13. Under guard and in various states of dress, Americans continue their march through Hallschlag. A medic and soldier with a white helmet cover—at far right in the previous photo—pass before the camera.

Germans shot sixty-seven Allied soldiers while they were surrendering or afterward. Evidently soldierly honor was not quite dead, for reportedly one young German refused to let the prisoners he was guarding be murdered. Naturally, the photographers did not record these shootings for the edification of the home folks.

During the initial heady days of the offensive, the war correspondents who accompanied the German advance west had a field day photographing American POWs (4–12). To the advancing infantrymen of the I. SS-Panzerkorps, the sight of these humbled Americans must have been welcome indeed after suffering Germany's retreat from France following the Normandy invasion and months of heavy Allied bombings of their Fatherland. The photographers' chance to show their own troops victorious and the would-be invaders of the Fatherland vanquished was all the more compelling. The thousands of prisoners and their captured equipment particularly fascinated the German photographers.

When taken prisoner, many Americans were not wearing the heavy clothing they would need in the harsh winter weather (4–13). German soldiers took articles of warm clothing, including gloves, from them.

The correspondents now turn their attention to their compatriots. The fact that the traffic shown in photo 4–14 appears to be moving at a crawl is no coincidence. By the

4–14. German Kübelwagens and a horse-drawn vehicle traverse the Siegfried Line between the villages of Scheid and Merlscheid. Note the array of *Höckerhindernisse* (literally "hump obstructions"), or dragon's teeth tank obstacles.

afternoon of 16 December, the main east-west thoroughfare through the Siegfried Line was jammed with vehicles due to a blown bridge near Losheimergraben.

On *Rollbahn* D late in the afternoon of 16 December (4–15), a paratrooper stands at one end of a bridge and watches a truck's entry. German engineers erected this particular bridge to span the Malmédy-Stadtkyll railroad cut. Later, the Germans themselves would blow up the bridge during their retreat from the area.

At about 1400 on 16 December, Obersturmbannführer Peiper and his column approached the site of this bridge. They stormed around the other vehicles on the road and somehow managed to gain the embankment on the other side—a not impossible task for tanks or half-tracks but quite difficult for regular trucks and other vehicles. The bridge was in place by 1600 and not a moment too soon for the vehicles idling in the backup that now extended a considerable distance to the rear (4–16).

4–15. While a junior grade officer (likely an engineer) lounges at left, German trucks cross the railway line between Stadtkyll and Malmédy via a Type-J replacement bridge. Note the camouflage on the top of the truck just entering the bridge's east side.

4–16. After riding across the J bridge, the photographer pivots and snaps a picture of the column making its way over the replacement bridge. Set up as a prudent precaution, a 20mm Flak 38 antiaircraft gun mount guards the engineers' completed work.

4–17. German view of a U.S. P-47 fighter flying at low altitude east of Merlscheid.

4–18. Kübelwagen from *Kampfgruppe* Peiper bounces down *Rollbahn* D past a small church and a U.S. antitank gun near Merlscheid.

Continuing west on his journey down *Rollbahn* D, the photographer spots one of the strafing U.S. fighters that were the bane of the German armored columns (4–17). Particularly during the first days of the offensive, the Americans prayed for good flying weather while Hitler relied heavily upon bad weather for surprise and security.

As the column moves on, a vehicle passes an abandoned U.S. 76mm antitank gun, mired at right (4–18). Note the bare metal of the gun's breach. The Americans had not abandoned the weapon without a fight, as evidenced by the damaged armor on its right side (4–19).

The American POWs' dreary march continued to pro-

4–19. The war correspondent backtracks approximately fifteen steps to get a better photograph of the antitank gun.

4–20. The American prisoners from the 99th Infantry Division trudge to the rear on the road between Lanzerath and Merlscheid.

4–21. The guard at far right in the previous picture passes before the camera.

4–23. A shocked American prisoner casts an empty glance at the camera.

vide enticing material for the photographers. Here a German paratrooper from the 3. Fallschirmjäger-Division, armed with a Mauser rifle and equipped with an entrenching tool, leads this particular file of prisoners wearing various states of dress. Another guard marches along the column at far right (4–20). This soldier, wearing a white camouflage helmet cover, is armed with a Walther P-38 pistol (4–21). Gunfire off to the right has attracted the men's attention. Some of the prisoners glare at the photographer in stunned silence. In this group, most are fortunate in being clad in overcoats and galoshes—and in being alive (4–22). Some men, however, could not conceal the depths of their dejection (4–23).

4–22. American prisoners glare at the *Kriegsberichter.*

4–24. A *Königstiger* with its 88mm gun pointing skyward clanks down the road toward Lanzerath while U.S. 99th Division POWs pass in the opposite direction. Note the checkerboard divisional patch on the sleeve of the private first class at far right.

4–25. More POWs trudge down *Rollbahn* D toward Merlscheid.

The Tiger II, or *Königstiger,* at left in photo 4–24 is from the schwere SS-Panzer-Abteilung 501 commanded by Obersturmbannführer von Westernhagen. His vehicles brought up the tail end of *Kampfgruppe* Peiper. While with Peiper's armored force, the *Kriegsberichter* is now obviously tucked safely away at the column's rear.

Wheeling to the right, the correspondent photographs the same Tiger (4–25) as in the previous photo. Two motorcyclists armed with MP-40s follow behind. The tank crewman at the right wears the black cap with the SS eagle, part of the special black uniform for armored vehicle crews.

The action here (4–26) takes place near Roth. Of the U.S. garrison there, three men were killed and eighty-seven surrendered. In the aftermath, a jackbooted *Luft-*

4–26. German soldiers from the 18. Volksgrenadier-Division, 5. Panzer-Armee, near Roth rummage through the camp of the U.S. 14th Cavalry Group, which was attached temporarily to the 106th Infantry Division.

4-27. The correspondent follows two other soldiers into camp.

4-28. An SS infantryman examines an abandoned U.S. M45 quadruple machine-gun mount belonging to the 413th AAA Battalion, attached to the First Army.

waffe soldier in a camouflage smock, probably from the 295. Volksgrenadier-Regiment, tramples blankets and ration boxes pulled from the Americans' vehicle at right. Note that this soldier carries ammunition pouches only on the left side of his belt. In the background, another soldier walks out of the deserted camp after hitting the jackpot and finding two cans of gasoline. American tents still stand farther to the rear. The soldiers in their camouflage smocks proceed down a corduroyed road, while a man on the right collects jerricans (4–27).

Another soldier profiting from the ransacking action carries an extra pair of shoes and smokes what is likely an American cigar (4–28). The American crew of the pictured gun registered a tally of three kills on the mount before its capture. Extra ammunition boxes are stowed in the trailer. Photos 4–29 and 4–30 give a forlorn picture of the deserted U.S. camp. Note the camouflaged gear at the right, the scattered jerricans, empty cable reel, and the wooden door to the tent. Stove chimneys rise through the roofs of the tents. Cases for artillery shells are stacked at left (4–30).

4-29. U.S. enlisted billets at Roth.

4-30. Abandoned olive-drab tents contrast against the gray December sky.

4-31. Captured U.S. rations piled high in a German Kübelwagen.

4-32. The ignominy and impersonal brutality of war. *Luftwaffe* personnel loot American corpses at a crossroads in Honsfeld; note the barefoot American at far left. The German soldier at left appears to be putting something in his pockets.

On the move again (4–31), the correspondent speeds northwest, arriving in the Belgian village of Honsfeld in *Kampfgruppe* Peiper's wake. At an intersection in Honsfeld, the fenced enclosure at left is likely a small cemetery. The view looks back down *Rollbahn* D toward Losheimergraben (4–32), but the advance continued to the right toward Büllingen, a major U.S. supply point. The *Bahnhof* (train station) is one-half kilometer away at left.

In 4–33, the photographer walks forward, turns to the right, and presses the shutter release on his Leica to record American casualties at Honsfeld. *Luftwaffe* soldiers in photo 4–34 inspect captured U.S. vehicles and a 76mm antitank gun in a Honsfeld farmyard. Equally curious, two infantrymen explore an American M3 half-track mired in the mud off the road at left (4–35). Note the SS skull insignia on the cap of the man leaning out of the German vehicle at right. Camouflaged with evergreen sprigs, the SdKfz 251 mounts an MG42 on a trunnion in the rear as it rolls toward Büllingen.

The German Offensive Opens 63

4-33. American casualties from the fighting in Honsfeld facedown in the mud.

4-34. Triumphant *Luftwaffe* soldiers take a short breather. Note gas mask canisters carried by the soldiers at right and the bandoliered MG42 ammunition worn by the soldier at left.

4-35. An SdKfz 251 half-track proceeds through Honsfeld on its way toward Büllingen.

4–36. American dead near their 76mm antitank gun in Honsfeld.

When leaving Honsfeld for Büllingen, the Germans insisted that a sixteen-year-old girl show them the way. After the snow melted later in the year, her body was found beside the road. The Germans reached Büllingen before the defenders could mine the roads into town. Quite a few Americans managed to get away, but one battery had fifty-eight of its sixty-nine officers and men captured. A real find for the Germans was a stock of gasoline to fill their vehicles.

A final view of the Honsfeld area shows American soldiers left for dead at their post of duty (4–36) and two Germans tearing off on their motorcycle (4–37). This must have been a cold ride for the driver, who has lost his cap, perhaps blown off in the wind. Mud flaps protect his steering hand from the elements—the other hand is in his pocket. The passenger rides in back because a jerrican occupies the side-car.

Roll 2—18 December: The Advance Toward Trois Ponts; 1. SS-Panzer-Division—*Kampfgruppen* Knittel, Peiper, and Hansen; Kaiserbaracke, Ligneuville, and La Vaulx-Richard

4–37. Likely having just departed Honsfeld, two SS-*Kradschützen* press forward on their motorcycle. Note the "cat-eye" cover on the headlamp.

The location of this photographic sequence is Kaiserbaracke, a crossroads on *Rollbahn* E between Malmédy and St. Vith. While the company commander checks his map, the driver, seated and impassive at the right, seems not to be enthused with the photo opportunity he is providing the *Kriegsberichter* (4–38). At this point, vehicles and units from the various *Kampfgruppen* were very much mixed on *Rollbahn* E. Though giving the impression of a hard turn to the south, the roadway toward Recht

4–38. Seated in his Schwimmwagen, a company commander of SS-Panzer-Aufklärungs-Abteilung 1 (*Kampfgruppe* Knittel), possibly Obersturmführer Walter Leidreiter of 2. Kompanie, checks his map. Note the road sign knocked askew and the American "202 ORD DEPOT FWD" placard placed atop the signpost. The Schwimmwagen was an amphibious version of the Kübelwagen.

will soon turn almost due west. After passing through Recht, Hansen's column continued west toward Trois Ponts. Behind the truck in photo 4–39 is a late-production SdKfz 250/1 half-track mounting a machine gun and its shield. It appears to be headed straight through the intersection. A man is walking behind the half-track, just to the right of the truck.

The tank shown in photo 4–40 is from schwere SS-Panzer-Abteilung 501, Peiper's "tail-end Charlie." The "222" side number on the tank (not visible here) denotes 2. Kompanie (company), 2. Zug (platoon), second vehicle. Probably the slower-moving Tigers fell behind the rest of Peiper's *Kampfgruppe. Rollbahn* D, the road to which the Tiger IIs were assigned, was in terrible shape. Obersturmbannführer von Westernhagen likely decided that his sixty-eight-ton tanks might become mired in the

4–39. Vehicles from *Kampfgruppe* Hansen make a left turn toward the town of Recht. In front is a Steyr 1500 truck.

4–40. Loaded down with *Luftwaffe Fallschirmjäger,* Tiger II "222" from *Kampfgruppe* Peiper clatters northwest and straight through Kaiserbaracke on the way to Ligneuville.

4–41. Half-tracks of *Kampfgruppe* Knittel clank through Kaiserbaracke, bound for Ligneuville.

4–42. Cigar between clenched teeth, Ochsner poses in his Schwimmwagen beside the Malmédy and St. Vith road signs. Previously published versions of this and the two subsequent photos have often purported (in error) to show Obersturmbannführer Joachim Peiper.

4–43. A cooperative Ochsner, his driver, and Oberscharführer Persin check their map for the eager *Kriegsberichter*.

mud and opted for *Rollbahn* E. A noncommissioned officer (NCO) identified as Oberscharführer Persin, probably Obersturmführer Leidreiter's lead *Zugführer*, stands in the background at right, having just walked up behind the SdKfz 250/1 in photo 4–39 only moments before.

The vehicles shown in photo 4–41 are SdKfz 250 light half-tracks from SS-Panzer-Aufklärungs-Abteilung 1. As with the SdKfz 251 at Honsfeld, evergreen boughs adorn them. The SS runes have been painted out of the license plate on the vehicle at right, which has a towing cable attached to its front end. Two NCOs—Persin (at left) and Unterscharführer Ochsner, likely one of Persin's squad, or *Gruppe,* leaders—both carrying binoculars, stroll down the road. Note that the Malmédy road sign has been "repaired," or pulled back into position with a Mauser rifle slung over the sign's right end. The Ordnance Depot sign has also been removed. The Mauser "fix" to the road sign is obvious in photo 4–42. Note the mud-splattered vehicle and the cat-eye covers on the headlamps. Photographs 4–43 and 4–44 provide a touch of history à la carte as these Germans pause to pose for the ubiquitous photographer.

Along with the rest of schwere SS-Panzer-Abteilung 501, the tank pictured in photo 4–45 turned toward Ligneuville to rejoin the main body of *Kampfgruppe* Peiper to the north. The *Fallschirmjäger* aboard are armed with a variety of both German and captured weapons. At far left, one of the men carries a British Mk II Sten submachine gun. The paratrooper at center cradles an MG42 machine gun, while to his right, a man in a white scarf clutches his semiautomatic G43 rifle.

Perhaps in command of the squad of *Fallschirmjäger* on the tank is the Unteroffizier in the background at center

4-44. Chomping on what is probably one of Ochsner's cigars, the Schwimmwagen driver, a Rottenführer, mugs for the folks at home. This photo makes it obvious that the man at left is not Peiper. Peiper had finer features, a thinner face, and a cleft chin.

of photo 4–46. The paratrooper at right is similarly armed as the man accepting the light from the motorcyclist—with a G43. The ponderous weight of the sixty-eight-ton tanks has saved these men from any implication in the Malmédy massacre at Baugnez, as bad road conditions forced the heavy tank battalion to the south.

4-46. *Luftwaffe* personnel on the *Königstiger* accept a light for their cigarettes from an Unterscharführer on a motorcycle.

4-45. Loaded down with a host of *Fallschirmjäger*, a Tiger II rolls through the vicinity of Ligneuville between *Rollbahnen* D and E.

4–47. Sturmbannführer Gustav Knittel (*right*), commander of SS-Aufklärungs-Abteilung 1, and the commander of his staff company, Obersturmführer Heinrich Goltz, check maps at La Vaulx-Richard on the afternoon of 18 December.

4–48. A ruddy-faced Goltz glances uneasily at the camera, while Knittel, with binoculars, remains absorbed in his map board. Knittel's interwoven shoulder boards proclaim his rank of major in the SS. Goltz wears a leather overcoat over a camouflage smock and tunic while Knittel is in a waist-length leather jacket.

Having exhausted his photographic opportunities with *Königstiger* "222," the *Kriegsberichter* departed von Westernhagen's tank battalion and joined *Kampfgruppe* Knittel at the Belgian hamlet of La Vaulx-Richard. By this time Sturmbannführer Knittel's (4–47 and 4–48) column had been ordered to assist Peiper to the north. Gazing upward in photo 4–49, Knittel and Obersturmführer Heinrich Goltz appear to have heard the drone of aircraft engines.

Roll 3—17 or 18 December: On the Road West
1. SS-Panzer-Division—*Kampfgruppe* Knittel
Unknown Location

The following four exposures from this roll depict an unidentified unit (possibly *Kampfgruppe* Knittel) advancing. While the column waits for the word to go forward, two NCOs take a smoke break and sample American cigars (4–50). In photo 4–51, a *Grenadier* likewise enjoys an American smoke, but in his case a cigarette.

The terrible condition of the secondary thoroughfares of the Ardennes road net required an inordinate amount of time and manpower to accomplish routine tasks. To move a captured American jeep (4–52) called for no less than eighteen Germans. Another U.S. vehicle mired down the road to the right promises even more trouble. An American casualty is slumped over the wheel of still another vehicle in the background at right.

The road shown in photo 4–53 is typical of the type over which *Kampfgruppe* Peiper had to advance. Hence, the Tiger IIs of schwere SS-Panzer-Abteilung 501 detoured from *Rollbahn* D to E.

4–49. Knittel, binoculars in hand, and Goltz gaze up at the sky, likely having heard the arrival of the *Panzer* spearheads' worst enemy—the U.S. fighter-bombers of the Ninth Air Force.

4-50. Two SS NCOs, an Unterscharführer (*left*) and a Hauptscharführer (*right*), help themselves to a box of American cigars. Both men are in autumn-pattern smocks over field-gray tunics with their collars pulled up and out to display insignia of rank. Note the column of vehicles in the distance.

4-51. Infantrymen atop a Panzerspähwagen SdKfz 234/1 armored car rush westward during the breakthrough of the American lines. The inverted triangle left of the antenna is a hatch cover that folds down over the 20mm gun turret. Note evergreen camouflage.

4-52. How many *Grenadiere* does it take to move a captured American jeep? Probably directing the effort, the Hauptscharführer from photo 4–50 stands at center behind the radio-equipped jeep. Note the mix of overcoats and occasional camouflage smocks. A few of the soldiers have turned their hats around backward or pulled their earflaps down.

4-53. An SS antitank platoon (see the men in the middle distance) armed with Panzerschrecken, or "bazookas," traverses muddy, snow-covered roads during its advance into Belgium. A Kübelwagen and armored car are just visible in the background at left.

4–54. Three SS *Grenadiere,* two armed with Mausers, press south alongside the road leading to Poteau while a photographer stands outside a barbed-wire fence to record the action. Another *Kriegsberichter* stands at right with a motion picture camera. The photographer next will move down past the evergreen tree at far left. Note the abandoned U.S. jeep just beyond the correspondent and the M8 Greyhound armored car at left, barely visible through the fog.

4–55. Upon reaching the M8, an SS man climbs through the barbed-wire fence away from the road and snags his coat.

Roll 3 Continued; Roll 4—18 December: Clash with U.S. 7th Armored Division CCR
1. SS-Panzer-Division, *Kampfgruppe* Hansen North of Poteau

On 18 December, elements of *Kampfgruppe* Hansen passed through Recht and pressed their attacks southwest down the road leading to Poteau. One kilometer north of that small village, the Germans encountered a U.S. convoy (a portion of the 14th Cavalry Group assigned to the 7th Armored Division CAA) headed northeast. Finding themselves under attack and overwhelmed, the Americans panicked and fled, leaving their abandoned and burning vehicles filling the road.

The situation was made to order for at least two *Kriegsberichter* who accompanied SS-Panzergrenadier-Regiment 1. Men from the regiment's first battalion arrived soon after the Americans left. With the damp, foggy weather providing a dreary, gray backdrop, the road

choked with many burning enemy vehicles was a war correspondent's dream come true. The correspondents made the most of their opportunity, perhaps on the heels of real action at first, but then producing and directing several *ersatz* action scenes. The photographers—one with a 35mm Leica, the other with a motion picture camera—traversed a path alongside the road for perhaps two-hundred yards. After putting in a new roll of film, they recorded combat "action" while walking back from whence they came.

Through the work of noted historian and researcher Jean Paul Pallud, the precise stretch of road where these photographs were taken has been known for some years. Nonetheless, these photos are published here for the first time in their proper order. While it is disappointing to realize that much of the action shown here is staged, it is still interesting to observe the SS photojournalists plying their trade for the benefit of remote posterity.

In photo 4–54 we see two of these photographers at work, although the fog presented far from ideal conditions. They catch an SS man climbing through a barbed-wire fence (4–55). His reason for moving through the barbed wire becomes obvious in photo 4–56. The *Kriegsberichter* wanted to follow what was possibly the end of the real action, which moved out into the open and east of the road (4–57).

4–56. Safely through the fence, two *Grenadiere* attack some twenty yards south of the road.

4–57. The attack moves forward and to the left, toward a small grove of trees.

Photo 4–58 follows the *Grenadiere.* The man with the binoculars and the bandaged hand from 4–55 presses down the road at center, followed by his Mauser-toting comrades. Here the photographer has moved back to the road to record the men advancing just south of the road embankment. He snapped the right photo in this collage first and then pivoted to the left to take another. Thus, the first and third *Grenadiere* (from left to right) are actually the same person. This terminates the real action, if indeed any of the action recorded by the photographers was real.

4–58. The *Grenadiere* press forward past the wrecked jeeps and half-tracks of the 14th Cavalry Group.

4-59. An Untersturmführer (*left*) and Rottenführer rest from the day's labor under a U.S. M8 Greyhound armored car.

4-60. Across the road from the M8's safe haven lie other U.S. vehicles, burning and abandoned.

After taking the photos contained in the panorama, the photographer pivots left and walks perhaps ten steps to record two men resting underneath an American vehicle. Photo 4–59—most interesting because of its clarity—shows in great detail the officer in his woolen gloves, autumn-pattern camouflage parka, and field-gray M1943 cap (*Einheitsmütze*). Though hidden in the shadows, the Rottenführer wears a captured U.S. raincoat and is the proud bearer of the Iron Cross 1st Class, Infantry Assault Badge, Close Combat Clasp, and ribbons for either the Iron Cross 2d Class or the Russian Front Medal.

Across the road, several jeeps, M3 half-tracks, and other vehicles are burning (4–60). However compelling this photo is, the *Kriegsberichter* was only setting the stage for the next series of photos. The first of these feature the Rottenführer from photo 4–59. He "advances" out of the smoke (4–61 and 4–62), resplendent in his decorations and ribbons. The Germans had a penchant for wearing these into combat, even when their presence resulted in increased visibility to the enemy. To his right are the two Mauser-toting *Grenadiere* from the collage in photo 4–58. At far left, an infantryman armed with an MP43 likewise advances. After this shot, the cameraman once again crossed the road to take advantage of the props and scenery left behind by the Americans, where the Rottenführer obligingly orders his men to attack to the northwest (4–63).

The photographer now steps back from the site of the previous photo and pivots to document the sad state of a

4-63. Posing again, the Rottenführer orders an imaginary attack across the road to the northwest.

4-61. The Rottenführer of photo 4-59 retreated up the road some distance so that he may be seen "advancing" to the south.

4-62. The Rottenführer emerges from the smoke with his decorations and badges clearly visible.

4-64. A jumble of U.S. vehicles clogs the road to Poteau. Note the machine gun mounted atop the M3 half-track.

4-65. The *Grenadier* at left in photo 4-61 steps into the camera's sight to lead an attack but in the wrong direction, or northeast, back toward Recht. Although staged, this is a superbly composed shot of an enlisted man and his equipment—a shelter quarter tied onto his back, an entrenching tool and map case suspended from his belt, and an MP43 (or StG44) assault rifle in his hand.

U.S. jeep and half-tracks. These are the same vehicles seen in photo 4-58. Now the *Grenadier* shown at left in photo 4-61 takes his turn in attacking, but in the wrong direction (4-65). The scene is reminiscent of the lumbering Rottenführer's advance in photos 4-61 and 4-62, as the same M3 half-track burns in the background. Again the *Grenadier* moves forward, this time in the right direction (4-66).

Tiring of this game, the correspondent's first group of anonymous "actors" have pressed on, their fate forever unknown. Bereft of actors and having exhausted his photographic possibilities near the burning half-tracks, the photographer goes farther south to examine other American vehicles (4-67). Moving to the opposite corner of the M8 in photo 4-67 (which still shows at right), the *Kriegsberichter* looks back to the northeast, runs out of his first roll of film, and then reloads. From this photograph, one can see that the Americans had just enough time to unhitch the antitank gun at the center and to abandon the M5 Stuart light tank just in sight at the left (4-68).

Soon after changing his roll of film, the photographer crawls under the M8 and greets the arrival of another group of soldiers. Composed of SS men and *Fallschirmjäger,* the first man photographed was a paratrooper squad leader (4-69).

4-66. The infantryman from the previous photo advances toward Poteau from the same position but now in the correct direction.

4–67. Looking south toward Poteau, the orientation of the U.S. armored car's turret (*right*) documents the likely direction of the initial German attack that precipitated the American panic. The marking on the M8 at right, "1A 18C," indicates that the armored car belonged to the 18th Cavalry Reconnaissance Squadron, which was assigned to the First Army. Note the vehicle's tires are equipped with snow chains.

4–68. View looking back up the road toward Recht.

4–69. A *Luftwaffe* Unteroffizier armed with a captured M1 carbine advances south along the road embankment.

4–70. Recruited as actors, SS infantrymen press to the north, "advancing" the wrong way down the road toward Recht instead of Poteau.

4–71. A handsome, heavily armed *Grenadier,* tousled hair sticking out from under his helmet, pauses for the camera.

After coaxing (or ordering) the troops seen in photo 4–70 to stage a mock advance to the north, the *Kriegsberichter* emerges from behind the M8 armored car to gather more "action" shots for the propaganda machine back home. SS man 1 (note the eagle on his sleeve) carries an MP40. Just to his right, SS man 2 apparently, at some point in the past, has suffered a disfiguring facial wound under his left cheek. A *Fallschirmjäger* armed with a Kar 98k carrying ammunition boxes and an entrenching shovel stuffed in his belt, advances in the background. Handsome young SS man 3, armed with a knife and bandoliered with a 7.92mm ammunition belt for his MG42, poses for the correspondent while the paratrooper stalks away from the camera (4–71).

In photo 4–72 the soldiers move back, perhaps in the cameraman's effort to reset the shot in photo 4–70 for another take from the same position. This time the personnel are somewhat different—SS man 2, the paratrooper, and SS man 4 with a grenade under his left arm. "Extras" milling aimlessly in the background, however, ruin the effect.

Evidently tired of this occupation, the men take a break (4–73). SS man 3 and 5 and the *Fallschirmjäger* pause. SS man 3 pulls out a Browning pistol, while the paratrooper stands ready to dig a foxhole with the "E" tool stuffed under his Mauser 7.92mm ammunition pouches. SS man 2 lights up, likely with a highly prized American cigarette (4–74). Perhaps self-conscious about his wound, he has turned his right side to the camera. The image of SS man 1 (a *Sturmmann*) is particularly clear, showing the autumn

4-72. Reset and try again. The soldiers back up for another staged advance toward Recht.

4-73. Enough acting—it's time for a smoke break!

4-74. More cigarettes for the men of the SS-Panzergrenadier-Regiment 1.

4-75. SS troops savor the fruits of victory on the road to Poteau. (*Left to right*) SS men 2, 1, 4, 3, and 5.

4-76. Their break over, the soldiers begin to advance, this time, at least, in the right direction.

4-77. At the photographer's behest, three *Grenadiere* launch an impressive, if very much staged, attack to the north.

The German Offensive Opens

pattern of his outer tunic to great effect. Poised for action, he retains one MP40 magazine in the ready position under his belt. He wears an M1943-pattern helmet that was made with an outward crimp on the rim to ease the manufacturing process. In photo 4–75, SS man 3 still holds his Browning pistol and MG42. His hands are full, so a comrade must have lit his cigarette.

After the break, the *Kriegsberichter* once again crawls under the M8 Greyhound to photograph another advance (4–76). SS man 1 is almost out of the photo at left; his shelter quarter is showing. SS man 4 walks at center, grenade still stuffed under his arm, while SS man 2 advances at an oblique angle away from the road. Launching the attack, SS men 1, 4, and 2 dash across the road to the safe haven of the other side, only to have the photo ruined by a fourth man, indifferent to the photographer's best efforts, standing nonchalantly in the ditch at left (4–77).

Nearly halfway through the roll of film, the photographer gets a close-up of SS man 3 (4–78). The *Kriegsberichter* walks back toward the head of the American column—likely where his vehicle is parked—up the road toward Recht and accompanied by SS men 2, 1, and 3. Now engaged in a retrograde movement to the north, the photographer crosses the road to take advantage of the dramatic billow of smoke belching from the burning

4–78. SS man 3 gets one last close-up for the home front and one last opportunity to loot American treasure, yielding a tin of rations (as prized as American cigarettes) from an armored car.

American vehicles, the scene of the dramatic advance of the Rottenführer of photos 4–61 and 4–62 (4–79).

After trotting twenty yards or so closer to his point of origin, the war correspondent again turns and presses the shutter release on his Leica (4–80). One soldier on foot

4–79. SS men 2, 1, and 3 accompany the photographer back to his vehicle, "advancing" as they go.

4–80. SS men 2 and 1 continue the advance against the backdrop of burning American vehicles.

4–81. Troops move north at the scene of the skirmish depicted in photos 4–54 and 4–55.

4–82. Two officers, one of whom is possibly the commander of the company currently in the area, pass the photographer.

and another driving a captured U.S. jeep rush to get in position for one last action sequence (4–81), which is held up momentarily by two officers ambling through the *Kriegsberichter's* field of view (4–82). The photographer captures one last staged attack. The man in the distance at left facing the camera apparently has not received word that an "attack" is under way (4–83).

No doubt the photographer found his last two shots rather dull, after having enjoyed a short fling as a director. The men of SS-Panzergrenadier-Regiment 1 are finally on their way, and the next element of *Kampfgruppe* Hansen—the tank killers of SS-Panzerjäger-Abteilung 1—moves forward toward Poteau (4–84). His last shot is of guns moving into firing position (4–85). These Bison self-propelled guns (15cm S.I.G. 33/1 heavy infantry guns) are mounted on a Czech PzKpfw 38(t) chassis.

4–83. The SS troops stage one last advance to the south while exiting from the scene.

4–84. A Jagdpanzer IV/70 bypasses the American logjam ahead by moving off onto the south side of the road.

4–85. Two self-propelled guns are moved into firing position.

CHAPTER 5

German Special Operations, Massacre at Baugnez, Americans React to the Offensive

OPERATION GREIF

When planning *Wacht am Rhein,* Hitler was greatly concerned that Generalfeldmarschall Model's *Heeresgruppe* would not be able to reach the vital bridges across the Meuse while they remained intact. Without bridges, it could not cross and advance toward Antwerp. Operation *Greif,* or "Griffin," germinated from Hitler's idea to capture the bridges across the Meuse before the Americans had the opportunity to demolish them.

As developed, Hitler's proposal involved entrusting the 150. Panzer-Brigade to Obersturmbannführer Otto Skorzeny, SS commando extraordinaire (5–1). Taking advantage of the chaos during the anticipated breakthrough and using a mixture of captured U.S. and disguised German vehicles (5–2 and 5–3), the brigade would "retreat" toward the Meuse. Then it would secure the bridges, enabling Model's two armies to cross the last great natural barrier between the *Wehrmacht* and Antwerp.

Although the idea itself was splendid, the Germans allotted insufficient time prior to the offensive to secure the right personnel and the vast quantities of captured U.S. gear and equipment required for such an operation. Moreover, while they did have many captured vehicles, these were widely dispersed and frequently not in the best running order.

To compensate somewhat for the lack of U.S. tanks and armor, the Germans disguised their own vehicles, with some efforts proving more effective than others. Improvisations ranged from the very convincing—welding

5–1. Obersturmbannführer Otto Skorzeny, 150. Panzer-Brigade and leader of Operation *Greif,* shown here as a Hauptsturmführer. This photo is one of several portraits of Skorzeny by Hitler's photographer, Heinrich Hoffmann. Although it has been published several times, this is the first instance where it has been used unretouched, showing Skorzeny's original rank. It was common practice for German war heroes to be "promoted" to their current rank in official photography. Note the prominent *Schmisse,* or dueling scars, on Skorzeny's left cheek.

5–2. A Sturmgeschütz from Hauptmann Scheff's *Kampfgruppe* Y that the Americans found abandoned at Geromont. Note the white star painted on the sides and front. The 291st Combat Engineers removed a bobby trap from the vehicle on 15 January 1945.

5–3. After the explosion of an incendiary grenade that Skorzeny's retreating commandos had planted, a booby-trapped SdKfz 250 light half-track from the 150. Panzer-Brigade burns in Regne, Belgium. As with the brigade's other vehicles, this one was painted olive drab and adorned with the obligatory white stars.

5–4. An American military policeman (MP) checks the papers of a Belgian civilian near Bastogne on 21 December.

sheet metal onto tanks to simulate the angular profiles of U.S. tank destroyers—to those less than convincing, such as painting crude white stars on unmodified German vehicles. The paper strength of Skorzeny's brigade was also considerably higher than what was available on the eve of the offensive. With insufficient personnel and equipment, Skorzeny prudently scaled back his *Panzer* brigade from three to two battalions.

The brigade itself turned out to be a hodgepodge of SS commandos, paratroopers, and volunteers from all branches of the service. To provide some measure of unit cohesion, Skorzeny obtained two *Luftwaffe* paratrooper battalions and miscellaneous armored vehicle and tank crews from nearby *Panzer* and *Panzergrenadier* divisions. Organized into three *Kampfgruppen*—X, Y, and Z—the troops were to move forward with the 1. and 12. SS-Panzer-divisions and the 12. Volksgrenadier-Division.

Working in tandem with Skorzeny's brigade were the men of *Einheit* (unit) Stielau (named for its leader, Hauptsturmführer Stielau), 150 of the best English-speaking troops from among those selected for the operation. Dressed in U.S. uniforms and riding in jeeps, they were to spread as much confusion as possible behind enemy lines by blowing up bridges and supplies, disrupting communications, removing road signs, redirecting traffic, and disseminating false orders. The remaining volunteers were assigned to the 150. Panzer-Brigade.

As unconvincing as many of *Einheit* Stielau's commandos might have appeared, clad as they were in incomplete American kit, they did succeed in spreading panic and confusion of the highest order behind the American lines. Enough horror stories circulated concerning the German wolves in sheep's clothing that the extra security measures put into place to deal with the menace delayed U.S. troops far from Skorzeny's brigade or the commandos. Alleged spies and suspected saboteurs (those who honestly thought the Cubs *were* in the American League) were everywhere. These security measures seriously inconvenienced Belgian civilians as well as the Allied soldiers. With paranoia and fear spreading throughout the American lines, no one was above suspicion (5–4).

For the men of 150. Panzer-Brigade, the frustration of the traffic jams at Losheim and the failure of the 6. Panzer-Armee spearheads to penetrate as far as planned meant that their operation to seize the Meuse bridges was doomed almost from the start. Realizing the futility of pursuing their clandestine operation any further, Skorzeny obtained permission from Oberstgruppenführer Dietrich to assemble his three *Kampfgruppen* into a single unit to operate under the I. SS-Panzerkorps. Then, the brigade expended itself in the hard-fought battles of the Ardennes. Although staying in line through 28 December, the brigade eventually withdrew and disbanded, with all members in their original units by 23 January.

5-5. **A German soldier, partially clad in American clothing, lies dead in Hotton, Belgium. The hapless man's dog tags have been pulled out from his tunic, presumably as evidence of his misdeeds.**

Although the German columns never reached the Meuse, Hitler's concerns regarding blown bridges were fully justified, as the mounting frustration of *Kampfgruppe* Peiper would later attest. All too often during the campaign, the Germans arrived at a stream only moments after what Obersturmbannführer Peiper called "those damned engineers" had blown up the bridge.

A curious side effect of *Greif* was that many German soldiers who had "liberated" various articles of American clothing were summarily shot as spies when captured (5–5). The German lightweight smocks and their flimsy wool-rayon blend tunics and trousers were notoriously insufficient at keeping out the cold. The warm American clothing offered too great a temptation for many German soldiers and undoubtedly cost many their lives.

EXECUTION OF GREIF COMMANDOS SCHMIDT, BILLING, AND PERNASS

Skorzeny had been worried that any of his men captured while wearing U.S. uniforms might be treated as spies, but the lawyers who researched the problem advised him that the practice was within the rules as long as the men did not actually participate in combat. One wonders just how far this reasoning reassured Skorzeny, but he had his orders.

It certainly did not impress the Americans. All eighteen of Skorzeny's men who were captured were shot as spies.

Three of his commandos—Oberfahnrich (officer candidate) Günter Billing (also known as Charles W. Lawrence), Unteroffizier Manfried Pernass (Clarence van der Wert), and Gefreiter Wilhelm Schmidt (George Sensenbach)—were assigned to monitor the condition of the Meuse bridges, radio back that information, and await the arrival of Dietrich's 6. Panzer-Armee. Riding in a jeep and dressed in American uniforms, the trio easily penetrated the American lines and were stopped only when they went to Aywaille to cross the Amblève River. Unable to supply the correct password, they were apprehended and arrested for espionage.

Billing (the leader) and his comrades had between them a large quantity of U.S. and British currency and an odd assortment of German, American, and British weapons. Following a quick military trial at Henri-Chappelle, all three were found guilty of espionage and sentenced to death. They were executed on 23 December.

The cold was intense that day; one witness described the German prisoners as "blue with cold." Photos 5–6 through 5–10 show the inexorable progress of the execution. There is disagreement as to the Germans' last words. The official caption of photo 5–9 quotes Billing as shouting, "Heil Hitler und das Deutsche Reich!" One other witness remembered only, "Es lebe unser Führer, Adolf Hitler!"

5–6. Found guilty of espionage, *Greif* commandos (*left to right*) Wilhelm Schmidt, Günter Billing, and Manfried Pernass await their execution on 23 December. MPs secure the trio to shooting posts erected near the wall of the building behind. Schmidt cannot look at the firing squad. The bespectacled Billing stares unblinking ahead. Pernass, not yet tied to the post, looks to his leader, perhaps for inspiration or encouragement.

5–7. As MPs tie up Pernass, pulling his hands behind him, the convicted spy continues to look expectantly toward Billing.

5–8. With Pernass blindfolded and secured to the shooting post, Capt. Joseph Eiser, medical officer of the 633d Clearing Station, affixes a target for the firing squad (a four-inch white circle pinned over the heart). A grim-faced MP stands close by. Note that there are no bullet holes in the wall behind Pernass.

5-9. Startled Signal Corps photographer Cpl. Edward A. Norbuth flinches, blurring the photographic image, as the volley from the firing squad crashes into the three prisoners and the wall behind. Four riflemen were assigned to each convicted spy.

5-10. Gefreiter Wilhelm Schmidt pays the price of a failed mission.

Although the executioners were to aim at the victims' hearts, the four Americans assigned to Schmidt appear to have either been very upset by their task or taken exceptionally poor aim. At least one rifleman deliberately missed to the left. Perhaps, like the German guard at Honsfeld, he could not bring himself to kill a helpless man, even in the line of duty.

OPERATION STÖSSER

To supplement Skorzeny's commando operations, Hitler envisioned a second behind-enemy-lines operation involving a paratrooper drop to the north in support of Dietrich's 6. Panzer-Armee. After jumping in the Hohes Venn area in the predawn hours of 16 December—the offensive's first day—the airborne force, led by Oberst Freiherr Friedrich-August von der Heydte (5–11) of the 6. Fallschirmjäger-Regiment, would take control of the territory between Eupen and Verviers. Then it would secure the road net for Dietrich's army.

Like *Greif,* Operation *Stösser* (Hawk), as it was code-named, was a brilliant plan. As designed, it was capable of providing a certain amount of insurance for the 6. Panzer-Armee and of fomenting absolute chaos in the Americans'

5-11. Oberst Freiherr Friedrich-August von der Heydte, shown here as a major in 1943. A veteran parachutist and a certified German hero, von der Heydte commanded I./Fallschirmjäger-Regiment 3 during the legendary, if ill-fated, airborne assault on Crete.

Oberst von der Heydte did not learn of his assignment until 8 December, when he was summoned to the headquarters of Generaloberst Kurt Student of Heeresgruppe H. At that time he was informed only that the mission was to take place; no one disclosed a date or location. The *Luftwaffe* colonel was to be provided with a *Kampfgruppe* of eight hundred men. He could not use his own regiment, however, on the grounds that moving such a large body of troops might attract the attention of American reconnaissance and intelligence.[*] Instead, each airborne regiment of the II. Fallschirmkorps was to contribute one hundred men. Von der Heydte must have been keenly disappointed that he could not use his 6. Fallschirmjäger Regiment effectively. Although he was free to use his own leaders and officers, establishing unit cohesion within the new *Kampfgruppe* would be difficult, if not impossible, to achieve.

Predictably, the various components of the II. Fallschirmkorps failed to provide their best people for the mission. Instead, they emptied into the *Kampfgruppe* large numbers of men totally unsuited to the task at hand. Many of the so-called *Fallschirmjäger* had never even jumped out of an aircraft. Nor could Oberst von der Heydte count on experienced transport pilots to carry the men to their drop zone. Mirroring the *Luftwaffe*'s critical shortage of pilots, many were fresh from flight training and abbreviated training at that. They had not qualified in the Junkers Ju-52 transports (5–12) and were skilled in neither night nor formation flying.

rear. Unfortunately for the Germans, *Stösser* fell victim to the same maladies suffered by *Greif*—inadequate support in men and matériel, insufficient time for proper preparations, and poor execution.

[*]The assembly of Model's *Panzer* and *Volksgrenadier* divisions had done so. One wonders what difference another eight hundred men would have made.

5-12. A Junkers Ju-52 in winter camouflage wrecked when it attempted to land near Asselborn in northern Luxembourg. Although not associated directly with *Stösser,* this aircraft was from one of the transport groups supporting the operation. This particular aircraft and another have often been erroneously attributed to *Kampfgruppe* von der Heydte, when, actually, both aircraft landed in an attempt to service a German field hospital near Asselborn.

5–13. An American patrol from Company F, 3d Battalion, 1st Infantry Regiment, probes the Belgian woodlands in search of German paratroopers on 18 December 1944.

5–14. Men of the 3d Battalion, 18th Infantry Regiment, bide their time near Sourbrodt, Belgium, and wait for their comrades to flush *Fallschirmjäger* from the woods nearby on 19 December.

So, with an estimated 10 percent chance of success, *Kampfgruppe* von der Heydte awaited transport to the airfields in the early morning hours of 16 December. Unfortunately, the needed transportation failed to appear, so the jump was rescheduled for the next morning. Gone was their advantage of surprise. Then when the jump actually occurred, it went awry from the start. Although the hapless Ju-52 pilots undoubtedly did their best, of the *Kampfgruppe*'s seven companies—four light, one heavy weapons, one signal, and one supply—perhaps 450 men landed in the Hohes Venn vicinity. Only 100 men landed in the drop zone proper, and only 300 ultimately assembled with the *Kampfgruppe* during the next two days. Accentuating the poor performance of the *Luftwaffe* transport pilots, 250 men jumped near Bonn some fifty miles away.

With most of his force absent, Oberst von der Heydte changed his mission's thrust to reconnaissance, a role he pursued with remarkable success. However, the detailed information garnered by his *Fallschirmjäger* never made it to Dietrich and the 6. Panzer-Armee, for none of the *Kampfgruppe*'s radio sets survived the drop intact. Thus, the *Kampfgruppe* had to content itself with patrolling, destroying a few American vehicles, and capturing several prisoners.

Together with the *Greif* commandos' capture, reports of these German paratroopers operating behind American lines heightened the sense of insecurity among U.S. troops in the Ardennes. Naturally, tracking down these infiltrators became an urgent task (5–13 and 5–14).

Their one-day's food supply exhausted and their ammunition low (the *Luftwaffe* resupplied the group only with cigarettes and fresh water [5–15 and 5–16]), on 19 December Oberst von der Heydte decided to withdraw his *Kampfgruppe* toward the German lines. Striking the rear of the American lines on 20 December, the *Fallschirmjäger* endeavored to fight their way through. Perhaps one-third of the famished, weary German paratroopers reached their own lines. Von der Heydte collapsed from exhaustion in Monschau (5–17). Rather than starve, he finally decided to give up his hiding place and passed a surrender note in English to the Americans via a Belgian.

5–15. Near Sourbrodt, Pvt. Harry N. Newton of Detroit, Michigan, examines supply containers dropped by the *Luftwaffe* for Operation *Stösser* paratroopers.

5–16. American soldiers hold up German parachutes near Sourbrodt on 19 December, mute testimony to Operation *Stösser*. Silk parachute material accompanied at least one Ardennes veteran back to the States. Capt. Arthur D. Wenger, chaplain in the 76th Division and father to one of the authors, used the silk to make pajamas. Unfortunately, the dye in the silk had no more staying power than von der Heydte's paratroopers; the pajamas ruined a set of bedsheets the first night Wenger wore them.

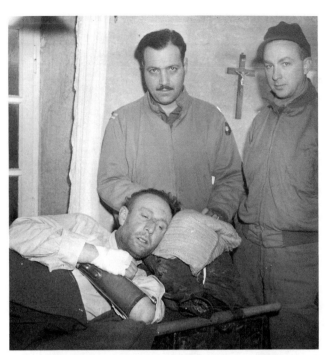

5-17. Receiving medical aid from Capt. Albert J. Haft and Lt. Col. John R. Woodruff, Oberst von der Heydte lies on a stretcher after he surrendered to 99th Infantry Division troops.

MASSACRE AT BAUGNEZ

More than any other event during the Ardennes Offensive, the massacre of American soldiers at Baugnez on 17 December 1944 (generally known as the Malmédy massacre because of its proximity to that larger town) came to symbolize the desperate nature of the struggle between the two great armies during December 1944. On the one hand, the Germans viewed themselves as fighting for their nation's very survival, and they were prepared to take any steps necessary to guarantee their success, including acts of the greatest barbarity. After the massacre, the Americans, on the other hand, were more convinced of the urgent nature of their mission to free Europe and the world from domination by a regime that would perpetrate such acts.

One somewhat curious but understandable aspect of the affair is the Americans' shock at the news of the Baugnez incident. Of course, anyone who had read the newspapers or listened to the newscasts since Hitler came to power knew that the Nazi regime was capable of savage and senselessly cruel acts. But perhaps the Americans still tended rather naïvely to associate atrocities with Nazis and expected better of German soldiers. Although the worst of the concentration camps, destined to arouse great disgust and revulsion in America, had yet to be liberated,

the Germans' checkered record in France, Norway, Russia, and other occupied areas should have dispelled any such illusions.

To the Americans, Malmédy had more immediacy than other German atrocities. For the first time, the victims were their own sons, brothers, and husbands. So the United States reacted with personal grief, horror, and fury, not just with impersonal moral outrage. It was almost as if the possibility of such an incident had never been entertained. Japanese barbarisms in the Pacific theater aroused revulsion but little surprise. But the perpetrators at Malmédy were German—a race from whom millions of Americans had sprung and whose culture, religion, and general outlook on life many Americans supposed to be similar to their own. Thus, this incident at an obscure crossroads in Belgium brought into focus for most Americans the true nature of a regime whose capacity for cruelty and inhumanity seemed to have no bounds.

An unfortunate chain of events, combined with the topography of the area, led to the massacre at Baugnez. As Peiper's *Kampfgruppe* pressed toward Stavelot on 17 December, the route over which he chose to lead his armored columns did not take a direct track to the west. Just west of Thirimont, a sizable hill separated it from the hamlet of Ligneuville. Although a country lane ran alongside the hill and connected with the main road to Ligneuville, Peiper probably judged that the poor condition of that secondary road might cost more time than if he stayed on the main road. So he cut north briefly, passed through the crossroads at Baugnez, and then proceeded to Ligneuville and points west.

Meanwhile, Battery B, U.S. 285th Field Artillery Observation Battalion, reached the town of Malmédy shortly before noon. On its way south to join the main body of the 7th Armored Division, to which it was assigned, Battery B on 16 December had been committed to the defense of St. Vith. Fighting its way through heavy American traffic in Malmédy, the convoy stopped at the command post of the 291st Engineer Combat Battalion. Its commander, Col. David E. Pegrin, did his best to dissuade Capt. Roger L. Mills, the column's leader, from taking the direct route south to St. Vith. Reports of German armor to the east near Büllingen prompted Pegrin to suggest instead that Mills backtrack through Stavelot and then proceed west. Faced with the prospect of losing his place in the divisional convoy and of adding perhaps one-third to the distance of his drive to St. Vith, Mills demurred. He proceeded on his original course, driving up the hill from Malmédy through Geromont to Baugnez. The Americans and *Kampfgruppe* Peiper were on a collision course (5–18 and 5–19).

At Baugnez, MP Pfc. Homer Ford, who was posted at the café-residence of Madame Adèle Bodarwé, saw Captain Mills's vehicles approaching from the west. The combat command reserve headquarters of the 7th Armored

5-18: Peiper's Fateful "Detour" to Ligneuville
17 December 1944

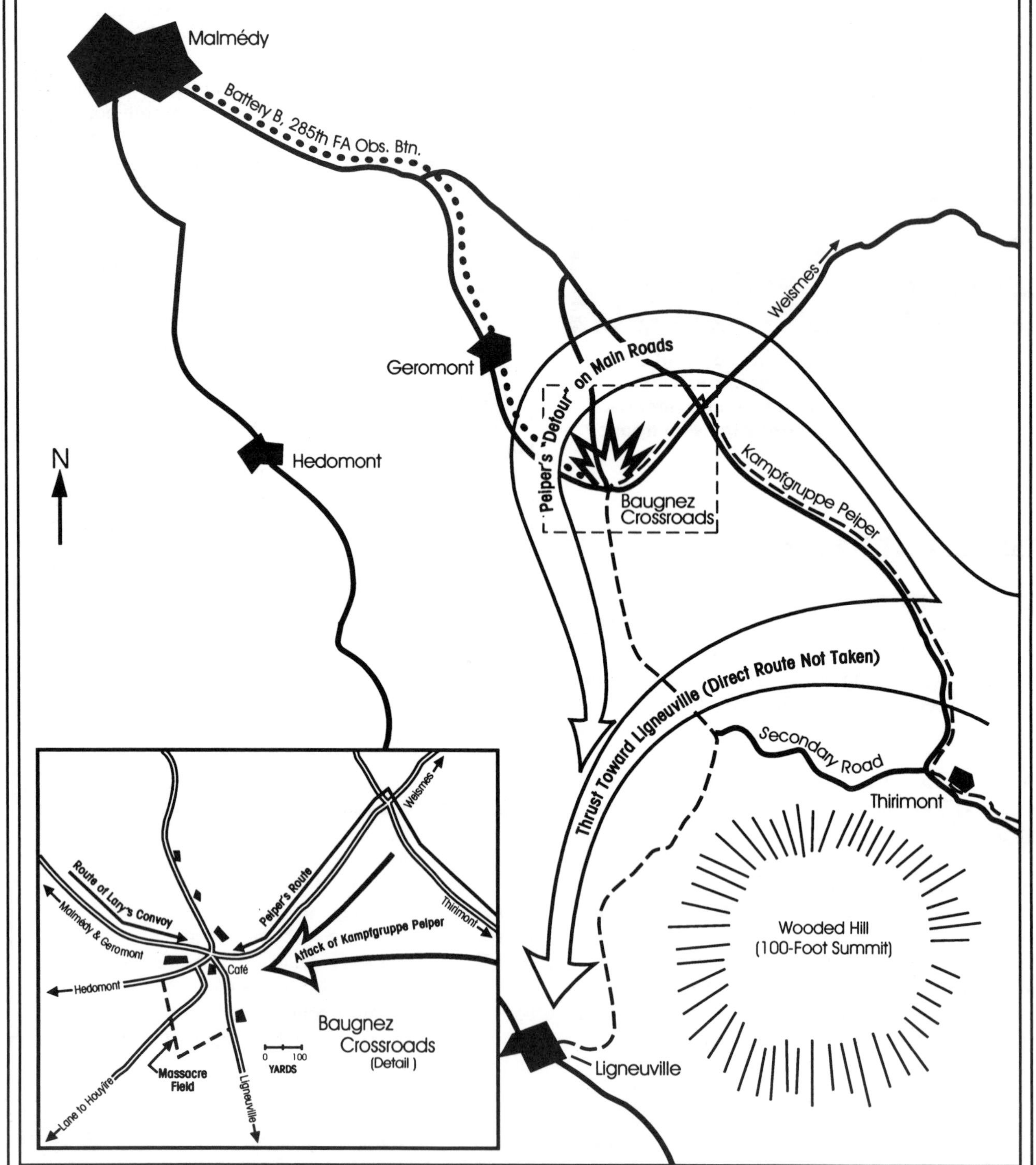

Malmédy

Battery B, 285th FA Obs. Btn.

Geromont

Hedomont

N

Welsmes

"Peiper's 'Detour' on Main Roads"

Kampfgruppe Peiper

Baugnez Crossroads

Thrust Toward Ligneuville (Direct Route Not Taken)

Secondary Road

Thirimont

Wooded Hill
(100-Foot Summit)

Ligneuville

Baugnez Crossroads (Detail)

Welsmes

Route of Lary's Convoy

Peiper's Route

Malmédy & Geromont

Thirimont

Attack of Kampfgruppe Peiper

Café

Hedomont

Massacre Field

Lane to Houvire

Ligneuville

0   100
YARDS

5-19. This view shows the U.S. convoy's final approach to the Baugnez crossroads, moving up hill east from Malmédy. Abandoned vehicles from Battery B, 285th Field Artillery Observation Battalion, still litter the side of the road.

had recently passed, turning right toward St. Vith. Ford directed the lead vehicle, a jeep driven by 1st Lt. Virgil Lary, to make the turn likewise (5–20). Suddenly the sound of gunfire thundered from directly ahead. Battery B's thirty vehicles had run squarely into the 1st Battalion of SS-Panzer-Regiment 1.

Predictably, Battery B proved to be no match for Peiper's powerful *Kampfgruppe*. Panic seized the Americans, many of who threw away their weapons and abandoned their vehicles in the road. The Germans bounced the Americans perfectly as 75mm shells screamed into the convoy, detonating among the U.S. vehicles. German in-

5-20. View at Baugnez looking due west down the roads that fork (*left*) to Hedomont and (*right*) down the hill to Geromont and Malmédy. The lead vehicle in the U.S. convoy was just about to make a right turn out of the photo at left toward Ligneuville and St. Vith. The truck at right, driven by Sgt. Alan M. Lucas, was actually the second vehicle in the convoy behind Lieutenant Lary's jeep. Note the house at left center, also visible in the previous photo. The ambulance at far right was driven by Pvt. Roy B. Anderson.

5–21. This view greeted the vehicles of *Kampfgruppe* Peiper as they approached Baugnez perhaps one hundred yards from the crossroads. A shed belonging to Henri LeJoly lies on Highway N23 (the road to Ligneuville) at left. The U.S. column was just behind the line of trees at right.

5–22. Commander of I./SS-Panzer-Regiment 1, Sturmbannführer Werner Pötschke, shown earlier in his career as a Hauptsturmführer. Perhaps a convenient scapegoat, Pötschke was killed in Hungary during March 1945 and thus could tell no tales or provide any rebuttal regarding the massacre.

fai nen dismounted their tanks and attacked from east to w st, down the main road, and across the fields east of Baugnez.

With his column in disarray and many of his men in flight, Lieutenant Lary saw that further resistance was futile. He ordered the men to cease firing and prepare to surrender. Some men hid in ditches and in the mud. Others, including MP Ford, sought shelter behind the café. The Germans found these men and herded them together with the surrendered main body. After searching the prisoners, the SS *Grenadiere* escorted the *Amis* into an open field adjacent to the café and just north of the road that led west out of Baugnez and toward Hedomont.

Supposedly, Peiper himself arrived during this time. He was visibly furious over the wrecked American trucks and their erstwhile intact fuel supply, both of which he could have put to good use. Time was short, however, so Peiper pressed on, allegedly shouting to the captured Americans as he passed, "It's a long way to Tipperary, boys!" He bounced down the road to Ligneuville (5–21),

leaving another officer—reportedly battalion commander Sturmbannführer Werner Pötschke (5–22)—in charge of the scene.

Exactly what followed next is uncertain. The Americans were lined up in eight rows in the field and faced a column of armored vehicles from 7. Kompanie, SS-Panzer-Regiment 1. A pistol shot rang out, fired by Sturmmann Georg Fleps, the assistant gunner on PzKpfw IV "731", supposedly with prior encouragement from his company commander, Hauptsturmführer Oskar Klingelhöfer, and under direct orders of his tank commander, Hauptscharführer Hans Siptrott.

Understandable disorder among the Americans ensued, followed by other pistol shots. Perhaps some of the prisoners appeared to break and run at this point, prompting uneasiness and panic among the SS soldiers. Then one of the Germans screamed the order, "Macht alle kaputt!!" [Kill them all!] Machine guns and machine pistols opened up on the rows of Americans prisoners until all had either run away or fallen on the ground (5–23).

5-23. The killing field. The Bodarwé café and the U.S. convoy lie some distance behind the photographer. Highway N23, *Kampfgruppe* Peiper's exit route from the scene, runs toward Ligneuville between the rows of trees at left. Also visible at left is the shed of Henri Lejoly, a Belgian witness to the massacre.

5-24. The burned-out ruins of Madame Adèle Bodarwé's house and café seen from the east. Peiper's *Kampfgruppe* would have advanced straight toward the café in the distance behind the trees at center.

5-25. Henri Lejoly, civilian witness to the massacre, played a far from heroic role. In the Bodarwé café at the time, he waved a welcome to the Germans and a little later pointed out the hiding place of some Americans. Even so, the Germans prepared to kill him because he had witnessed the massacre, but after a time let him go.

As *Grenadiere* from Klingelhöfer's 7. Kompanie cut down those who attempted to run away, a certain number sought refuge in Madame Bodarwé's café. The Germans set it on fire and shot the occupants as they emerged from the burning building (5–24, 5–25, and 5–26). The *Kampfgruppe*'s 9. Pionier-Kompanie now clattered onto the scene and found itself detailed to stay behind for a time to ensure that the Americans were all dispatched. For what must have seemed an eternity for those few survivors feigning death, the engineers walked among the fallen Americans, kicking the bodies and sending round after round into any form showing signs of life. When at last the Germans were satisfied that all prisoners were dead, they departed, turning south down the road to Ligneuville (5–27). They left the murdered Americans where they lay.

Shocked and wounded survivors, who ran or remained still and eluded the watchful eyes of the German engineer troops, struggled back to the American lines to tell a gruesome, and sometimes incoherent, story. The news was immediately and widely circulated among the American troops. Undoubtedly it served to stiffen resolve among the beleaguered Americans in the Ardennes. However, none of the stories that came through channels—either official or unofficial—prepared the Americans for what they would find southwest of the crossroads at Baugnez on 14 January.

5-26. View from the east window of the house in photos 5-19 and 5-20, with the Bodarwé café at left and the corner of the massacre site at right.

5-27. Highway N23, the road by which *Kampfgruppe* Peiper continued its advance to Ligneuville. Note the N23 signpost at left and the shattered branches of the trees, perhaps damaged by German shellfire.

5–28. Men from Company C, 291st Combat Engineers, pose at Baugnez for a group photograph on 16 January 1945.

As soon as practical, troops were sent to the scene to find the bodies and identify the victims.[*] Men from Company C, 291st Combat Engineers (5–28), had the unpleasant task of combing the massacre site and surrounding area. Black soldiers from the 3200th Quartermaster Service Company drew the gruesome assignment of distinterring the victims' bodies for identification and reburial (5–29). The engineers used mine detectors to locate the American bodies, which by this time were buried under nearly a foot of snow (5–30 and 5–31).

5–29. Black soldiers from the 3200th Quartermaster Service Company, led by 2d Lt. F. J. Fraser (*second row, far right*).

[*]A team from the inspector general's section of the First Army accompanied troops from the 30th Infantry Division to the massacre field on 14 January and began the unpleasant task of locating the American dead. The deep snow shown here disputes the Signal Corps captions dating most of the photos shown as 17 December. Although the date is uncertain, the photos were probably taken much later, perhaps around 16 January, which would correspond with group photos taken of engineer/ service troops assigned to locate and disinter the massacre victims.

5–30. An engineer walks past the head of the U.S. convoy toward the massacre field, which is just out of the photograph at left. Jeeps head down the road to Hedomont, likely carrying more engineers. The "1A-285F0B B-2" marking on the GMC two-and-a-half-ton truck denotes second vehicle of Battery B, 285th Field Artillery Observation Battalion, assigned to the First Army. A Sherman tank stands next to the house in the background.

5–31. Using mine detectors, engineers work to locate the slain American soldiers. This scene is viewed looking south from the road to Hedomont.

5–32. After sweeping away the snow, an engineer uncovers the corpse of an American soldier.

5–34. Looking northeast toward Bodarwé's café, the photographer snaps the main group of Americans massacred at Baugnez.

Slowly the snow gave up its secrets, one by one (5–32 and 5–33). Each corpse was temporarily assigned a number in lieu of positive identification, which would come after dog tags and other effects had been examined. Victim no. 3 had been shot through the top of the head. In caption after caption on the Signal Corps file prints are words to the effect that "THIS EVENT HAPPENED," as if to convince unbelievers and those who might seek to rationalize the incident. But the Malmédy massacre was not an isolated happening. Similar slaughters of American prisoners occurred elsewhere during the offensive, such as Honsfeld, not to mention well over a hundred unarmed Belgian civilians—one, a child only four years old.

The panorama 5–34 shows the largest group of corpses, while photo 5–35 depicts two victims some distance away. These two could have been among those

5-33. The grisly task of locating the American bodies continues, with the second and third bodies uncovered.

5-35. Two American bodies lie approximately one hundred yards from the massacre site. The view is along the south side of the road to Hedomont, looking west toward the crossroads.

5-36. Two black soldiers carry a victim to a waiting transport vehicle. Private Anderson's ambulance is at left.

killed during the opening minutes of the lopsided skirmish between *Kampfgruppe* Peiper and the U.S. convoy, or they may have been cut down trying to escape.

After numbering and recording the location of the bodies, the site team removed them to a makeshift morgue for examination. There U.S. examiners worked not only to identify the dead but also to establish a legal case against the perpetrators (5–36).

AMERICANS REACT TO THE OFFENSIVE

Reading accounts of the early days of the Battle of the Bulge, it is all too easy to form a dismaying mental picture of unstoppable Germans, destroyed U.S. equipment (5–37), and American soldiers running like scared rabbits. While the Germans enjoyed some success on the battlefield, everything had a price. Each engagement, even if victorious, cost men and matériel that Germany could ill afford (5–38). From the start, individuals and groups of Americans fought valiantly and held up the invaders for the few hours that can help decide the ultimate result.

In photo 5–39 one such group prepares to meet the coming German breakthrough. Others move toward the

5-37. An army in retreat. Vehicles belonging to the 99th Infantry Division withdraw to the west through the town of Wirtzfeld during 17 December 1944. Vehicle markings indicate that the truck is from the 372d Field Artillery Battalion, the 99th Infantry's heavy 155mm battalion. An M10 tank destroyer covers the withdrawal.

5-39. American infantrymen of Company G, 23d Regiment, 2d Infantry Division, dig in along an embankment on 17 December.

5-38. Likely from *Kampfgruppe* Peiper, a PzKpfw IV lies turret upended, put out of action by a tank destroyer in Wirtzfeld—one hopes by the M10 in photo 5–37!

5–40. Men of the 26th Regiment, 1st Infantry Division, move up to meet the German thrusts threatening the town of Büllingen on 17 December.

enemy approaching Büllingen (5–40) and Butgenbach (5–41). Photo 5–42 provides evidence of the skill of American bazooka teams. Near the same location of Krinkelt, American GIs have the pleasure of accepting the surrender of a German tank crewman (5–43). The Germans suf-

fered an even more painful loss when the Americans set a gasoline dump turned roadblock on fire (5–44). The fuel-starved Germans coveted gasoline more than any other booty that might fall into their hands.

For some time, nature seemed to favor the Germans,

5–41. The 26th Infantry Regiment's 1st Battalion advances to repel German attacks near Butgenbach during 17 December. Note the destroyed railroad bridge in the background and the sign at left that cautions drivers about craters in the road.

5-42. Two Panthers of I./SS-Panzer-Regiment 12 in Krinkelt were eliminated by U.S. bazooka teams on 17 December. Note that the side armor plating has been blown loose.

5-43. A *Hitlerjugend* crewman of Panther "126" surrenders to the Americans south of Krinkelt on 17 December.

5-44. On 19 December the remains of a gasoline dump that the Americans set on fire as a roadblock north of Stavelot.

5–45. Troops of the 325th Glider Infantry, 82d Airborne Division, move up the road near Werbomont, Belgium, on 20 December in heavy fog.

providing the poor weather Hitler counted on so heavily. The skies over the Ardennes were overcast, severely limiting Allied air activity. Fog lay thick over the Belgian landscape (5–45) and restricted visibility to about one hundred yards. This gave the Germans, armed with more area-type weapons such as machine pistols, something of an advantage. American riflemen could not see far enough to put their markmanship to the test. Their tank destroyers, however, could go about their business as usual (5–46 and 5–47). For at least one unfortunate German, the war was over (5–48).

5–46. M36 tank destroyers plunge through the gloom near Werbomont in support of the 82d Airborne Division.

5-47. On 21 December, M10 crewmen from the 823d Tank Destroyer Battalion of the 30th Division pose beside their vehicle in Stavelot, Belgium, for Signal Corps photographer V. C. Calvano. The photo commemorates their destruction of four tanks belonging to *Kampfgruppe* Peiper.

5-48. Stavelot, 21 December. A dead SS *Leibstandarte* infantryman serves as a reminder of *Kampfgruppe* Knittel's drive through the town on 18 December. The Americans reoccupied the town three days later.

**5–49. An army convoy stops to rest in the snowscape of the Ardennes during
22 December.**

The photos shown in panorama 5–49 were taken on 22 December. With Christmas so near, whenever the soldiers' minds strayed temporarily from the nasty business at hand, their thoughts must have turned to the rugged beauty of the area and to homesick dreams of family. Wistful spirits might have brightened had they known that the date of the picture, 22 December, was only two days away from what would come to be considered the turning point in the battle. On 23 December the weather broke, permitting full-scale Allied air action. Threatened from both the ground and air, on 24 December General der Panzertruppen von Manteufel concluded that "the objective could no longer be attained."

THE FALL OF ST. VITH

As early as 17 December, Dietrich's attacks in the northern sector began to lose steam as the U.S. 1st and 2d Infantry divisions moved up to reinforce the 99th Infantry Division. Trouble was brewing likewise for Manteuffel's 5. Panzer-Armee farther south. Although initially the Germans were able to exploit their penetration into Losheim and capture a substantial portion of the 106th Infantry Division, Americans occupying the vital road center of St. Vith put up a steadfast defense and prevented the Germans from advancing.

At first, St. Vith's defenders consisted of a lone combat engineer battalion supported by a handful of infantry and a few antitank guns. Manteuffel's Panzer-Armee had only to move quickly to take an important road junction. Sensing the danger, however, the Ninth Army ordered its 7th Armored Division, commanded by Brig. Gen. Robert W. Hasbrouck, to bolster St. Vith's defenses. Although the 7th Armored was on the Dutch-German border one hundred kilometers from St. Vith, in a rapid move somewhat foreshadowing the 4th Armored division's later relief of Bastogne, the 7th completed the move in twelve hours. It went into action even as the division vanguard drove into the village.

The 9th Armored CCB and two infantry regiments from the 28th and 106th Infantry divisions joined the 4th Armored. The infantry regiments covered the southern approaches to the town, while the 9th Armored CCB covered the west. To the north were the 7th Armored CCR, CCA, and CCB. It was at this time that the CCA ran afoul of *Kampfgruppe* Hansen north of Poteau (see Chapter 4). By 20 December twelve thousand men and two hundred tanks were in position.

Fortunately, traffic jams and icy roads prevented the 5. Panzer-Armee from launching a coordinated attack until 21 December at 1100. With the Americans facing overwhelming odds, the town finally fell on 22 December (5–50). Nevertheless, for Manteuffel the victory must have rung hollow, because his forces had frittered away five precious days in front of St. Vith when they could have been racing for the Meuse River (5–51).

5–50. Snow-covered St. Vith during the American effort to retake the town on 24 January. Allied bombing while the town was in German hands resulted in the moonlike landscape seen here. Few buildings were left intact.

5–51. At XVIII Corps headquarters in Harzé, Belgium, Lieutenant General Hodges pins a Silver Star on Brig. Gen. Robert W. Hasbrouck for gallantry in action during the defense of St. Vith.

CHAPTER 6

Bastogne Besieged

THE 5. PANZER-ARMEE ATTACKS TOWARD BASTOGNE

Capturing Bastogne was of major importance to the German drive. The town commanded a network of highways that, when overtaken, would enable the Germans to pour troops and armor throughout a wide area and give them multiple tactical choices on the way to the Meuse. Moreover, the Germans knew that, as long as the Americans held Bastogne, the Allies would have a potential base for a counteroffensive. In moving on Bastogne, the invaders had to take the town quickly, however; they could not afford to tie up large numbers of men and armor in an all-out battle or long siege. It was imperative that they capture Bastogne before the Americans could move in reinforcements and make a major fight of it.

Major General Middleton, VIII Corps commander, decided to divert most of Maj. Gen. William H. Morris's (6–1) 10th Armored Division away from Bastogne to the south in support of the 4th Infantry's counterattack against the Germans. Providentially he also ordered the 10th Armored's CCB north on 17 December to help hold the vital Bastogne crossroads. These tanks would form a substantial proportion of the armored firepower that Brig. Gen. Anthony C. McAuliffe's garrison was able to muster during the siege.

On that same day, the 969th Field Artillery Battalion prepared to take position and support the 101st Airborne Division west of Bastogne (6–2). Two days later, von Lüttwitz's XLVII. Panzerkorps was busily engaged in surrounding and isolating Bastogne. The 110th Infantry Regiment had been cut off from its parent, Major General Cota's 28th Infantry Division. In photo 6–3, two "orphans" of the 110th Infantry seem to realize the seriousness of their position. In an attempt to stem the German

6-1. Maj. Gen. William H. Morris (center), commanding general, 10th Armored Division.

6-2. Guns of the 969th Field Artillery Battalion dig in to support the 101st
     Airborne Division. Here men work to unload 155mm howitzer shell cases
     from the ammunition truck at left.

6-3. 110th Infantry Regiment "orphans" from Maj. Gen. Norman Cota's 28th
     Infantry Division share worried expressions in Bastogne on 19 December.
     The soldier at left is armed with grenades and an M1 carbine. A
     broadside addressed to Bastogne's inhabitants is attached to the
     bulletin board behind the soldiers.

6–4. Troops of the 506th Parachute Infantry, 101st Airborne Division, move out from Bastogne.

tide, the 506th Parachute Infantry left Bastogne and headed north (6–4). On December 20, however, some heavy artillery had to evacuate and managed to do so just before the Germans completely encircled Bastogne (6–5). This same photo shows a column of M3 half-tracks going toward Bastogne to bolster the city's mobile defenses. Snow chains are on the rear tires of the truck at center.

At a roadblock near Wiltz, Luxembourg, a town to the east of Bastogne, men of Company B, 630th Tank De-stroyer Battalion (6–6), waited. Attacks would come that same day from elements of the 5. Fallschirmjäger-Division and *Kampfgruppe* Kunkel (6–7) of Oberst Heinz Kokott's 26. Volksgrenadier-Division. The men of Company B bought valuable time for the city's defenders. Armed only with rifles and carbines, they held off Kunkel and his men for several hours, allowing the U.S. garrison in Bastogne additional time to deploy and prepare.

6–5. Heavy artillery evacuates Bastogne during 20 December.

6–6. Men of Company B, 630th Tank Destroyer Battalion (sans M36s), armed only with rifles, dig in at their roadblock near Wiltz.

6–7. Major Rolf Kunkel, *Kampfgruppe* leader, 26. Volksgrenadier-Division, shown here earlier in the war as a young Leutnant. Kunkel commanded his division's Aufklärungs-Abteilung 26.

"NUTS!"—ENCIRCLED BASTOGNE GETS RELIEF FROM THE AIR

On 22 December, German officers under the flag of truce brought a note from General der Panzertruppe von Lüttwitz, commander of XLVII. Panzerkorps, demanding the surrender of the Bastogne garrison. Maj. Alvin Jones delivered the note to Brigadier General McAuliffe (6–8) and his acting chief of staff, Col. Ned Moore. Upon reading the note, McAuliffe exclaimed disgustedly, "Aw, nuts!" After thoughtful deliberation, his staff agreed that McAuliffe's "Nuts!" was the perfect official answer to Lüttwitz's demand for surrender.

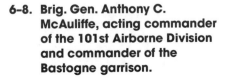

6–8. Brig. Gen. Anthony C. McAuliffe, acting commander of the 101st Airborne Division and commander of the Bastogne garrison.

6-9. Col. Joseph H. Harper, commander of the 327th Glider Infantry at Bastogne. He is shown here on 14 December 1951, when he was assigned to the 4th Infantry Division.

Col. Joseph H. Harper, commander of the 327th Glider Infantry (6–9), delivered and translated McAuliffe's "Nuts!" message to the Germans. Their arrogance and patronizing tone sent Harper into a fit of anger that he regretted afterward. He told the enemy emissary, Leutnant Hellmuth Henke from the *Panzer-Lehr*-Division, that in plain English "Nuts!" meant that the Germans could all go to hell. He informed Henke further that, if his commander insisted on pressing attacks, the Americans would "kill every goddamned German" who tried to break into the city. After telling Henke to be on his way, Harper incongruously wished the Germans "good luck." His German counterpart saluted stiffly, and both officers parted company in a huff.

The map (6–10) shows the state of the siege the day after the "Nuts!" incident. During the ten days of

6-10. The siege of Bastogne, 23 December 1944.

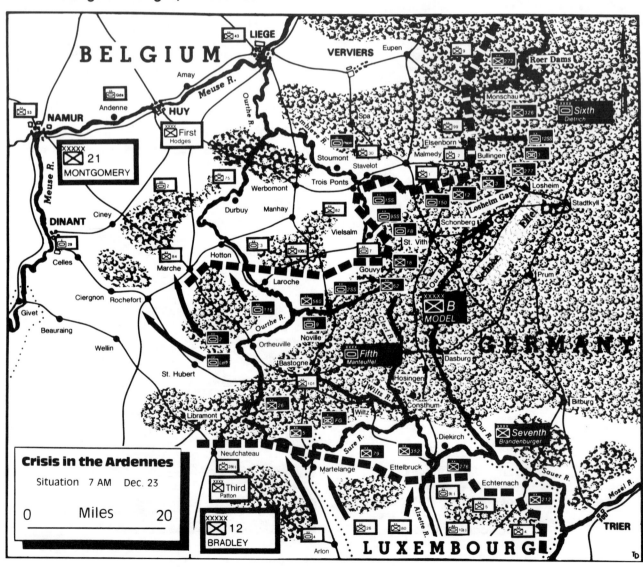

6–11. One of 241 C-47s from the IX Troop Carrier Command drops supplies for Bastogne one mile west of the town on 23 December.

Bastogne's isolation, air drops were the only available method of delivering supplies to the garrison (6–11). A fortuitous break in the weather on 23 December made large-scale air operations possible. Just before noon, air drops over the city began and continued late into the afternoon. The pressing need for ammunition was partly met, although the 101st Airborne was still critically short of M1 rifle ammunition and rounds for the 75mm howitzers and 76mm antitank guns. Other items dropped on 23 December included 16,488 single rations and a modest quantity of medical supplies.

On 24 December, 160 aircraft appeared over Bastogne with more ammunition (including for the M1 rifle), signal equipment, K rations, and gasoline. The workhorse of these air drops was the C-47 (6–12). Although these transports enjoyed the benefits of a strong fighter escort, they still had to deal with flak barrages from Lüttwitz's Panzerkorps. Moreover, repeated flights and the difficulty of maintaining the aircraft in cold weather increased the risks of mechanical trouble on the lumbering transports.

6–12. C-47 "Ain't Misbehavin'" after crash-landing near Bastogne. If the occupants of the small camp at right were present during the successful crash-landing, they certainly received the surprise of their lives. Invasion stripes, almost weathered away, adorn the C-47's fuselage.

6–13. Men of the 101st Airborne, many of them wounded, attend Christmas services even as the city is under siege.

CHRISTMAS IN BASTOGNE

The Bastogne garrison spent Christmas engaged in a wide range of activities. While some fortunate few attended religious services (6–13), most were busy maintaining the defense perimeter around the city. Still others waited for the much-needed air drops from the IX Troop Carrier Command, which was struggling to keep the garrison alive. One Signal Corps photographer, Tech. 5 Krochka, seemed particularly moved to record the day on film. Photos 6–13 through 6–17, as so many taken during the siege, are his handiwork.

Even with supplies coming in, the garrison was surviving the siege on a day-to-day basis. Christmas celebrations were likely far from the thoughts of the American defenders, most of whom were exhausted, wet, hungry, and cold. Officers of the 101st Airborne enjoyed a rather lean Christmas repast of what appears to be chicken, green beans, mashed potatoes, and coffee (6–14). Men of the 101st jumped rope in an effort to keep warm as they waited for the C-47 "Gooney Birds" to drop a shipment of medical supplies (6–15). Sure enough, supplies and ammunition dropped into Bastogne, perhaps one mile beyond the cemetery in the foreground of photo 6–16.

6–14. Christmas dinner at Bastogne for officers of the 101st Airborne. McAuliffe is seated fourth from the left. Ned Moore, his acting chief of staff, is seated at the left corner of the table. On the lower right corner sits Joseph Harper. The 101st Airborne's commander, Maj. Gen. Maxwell Taylor, is not present.

6–15. Airborne troops jump rope to keep warm on Christmas morning.

6–16. A most welcome Christmas present falls from a group of nineteen C-47s.

6–17. Soldiers, likely from Grenadier-Regiment 77, lie dead on the frozen ground where they fell on Christmas Day.

Christmas for the Germans was not any better, for death took no holiday (6–17). Oberst Kokott's 26. Volksgrenadier, together with *Kampfgruppe* Maucke, under Oberst Wolfgang Maucke (6–18), struggled to break through the American perimeter near Champs.

Despite the Americans' resupply effort in Bastogne, the Germans did not give up their siege. On Christmas Day, while Kokott's Grenadier-Regiment 77 attacked Champs, the PzKpfw IVs and StuGs of *Kampfgruppe* Maucke penetrated the lines of the 327th Glider Infantry and desperately tried to clear a way to Bastogne. The Christmas attack, which marked the Germans' deepest penetration into the Bastogne pocket, was finally repulsed by elements of Lt. Col. Steve Chapuis's 502d Glider Infantry and several tank destroyers. For his heroism during the action, Chapuis received the Distinguished Service Cross.

With the resupply effort breathing life into Bastogne's U.S. garrison, the Germans called upon the *Luftwaffe* to help break the back of the defenders. They mounted two separate heavy air raids on Christmas Eve, resulting in the destruction seen in photo 6–19. The day after Christmas, members of the 101st Airborne buried those comrades killed during the siege. With little open land available out of harm's way, the Americans had to make use of such plots as in the civilian cemetery shown in photo 6–20.

6–18. Oberst Wolfgang Maucke, *Kampfgruppe* leader, 15. Panzergrenadier-Division.

6–19. Bomb damage to Bastogne, 26 December 1944. After Christmas,
Tech/5 Krochka stayed on the job with his box camera, taking this and
the next two photographs.

6–20. In a civilian cemetery the day after Christmas, members of the 101st
Airborne Division bury their dead.

6–21. Two 101st Airborne members drag a parapack of badly needed medical supplies through the snow near Bastogne.

6–22. Two hapless Belgian civilians totter past a burned-out 10th Armored Division half-track near Bastogne on 27 December. Combined with the frigid, ice-covered terrain, carcasses of destroyed vehicles convey an air of forlorn desolation in the perimeter surrounding Bastogne.

BREAKTHROUGH: THE 4TH ARMORED DIVISION RELIEVES BASTOGNE

The Bastogne relief expedition that required such Herculean efforts was as much a tribute to Third Army commander Lieutenant General Patton as to the division itself. Patton was accustomed to asking his men to do the impossible on a routine basis. Taking on the determined, relentless character of their army commander, the men of the 4th Armored Division did what few thought was possible—disengage in the midst of a winter battle, move 150 miles toward an uncertain rendezvous, and relieve a sister division completely surrounded by the enemy.

Transferring from Maj. Gen. Manton Eddy's XII Corps to the II Corps on 19 December, the 4th Armored assembled in the Arlon sector on 20 December and moved forward to relieve Bastogne. After taking Martelange on 22 December, fighting the battle of Chaumont on 24–25 December, and pushing through Assenois to the outskirts of Bastogne on 26 December, the 4th Armored entered the city the next day.

The airlift that had made Bastogne's resistance possible continued (6–21). Although the initial priority was ammunition—particulary for artillery—other supplies soon began dropping into Bastogne. The sight of the C-47s droning over the city day after day must have been discouraging indeed for the Germans of the XLVII. Panzerkorps, as they watched their efforts to reduce the garrison go for naught. On 26 December, 289 C-47s took part in the supply mission with the loss of only one plane. German flak intensified considerably on 27 December,

and the supply effort lost thirteen aircraft out of 130. Gliders were also used by that time, braving the German anti-aircraft fire as they brought ammunition for the garrison's artillery.

All of this fighting had a devastating effect on the local civilians and their city (6–22). Although Maj. Gen. Hugh J. Gaffey's (6–23) 4th Armored Division would soon achieve breakthrough, this did not mean the end of hostilities in the Bastogne area (6–24). U.S. troops, vehicles,

6–23. Maj. Gen. Hugh J. Gaffey (*right*), commanding general, 4th Armored Division. This photo was taken after the war on 18 May 1945 in Neustadt, Germany. Major General Cota (*left*) of the 28th Infantry Division seems unimpressed by Gaffney, who by that time commanded the XXIII Corps. Perhaps he was bored by the mundane discussion that centered on the transfer of local German government functions to local units.

6–24. The relief of Bastogne, 26 December 1944.

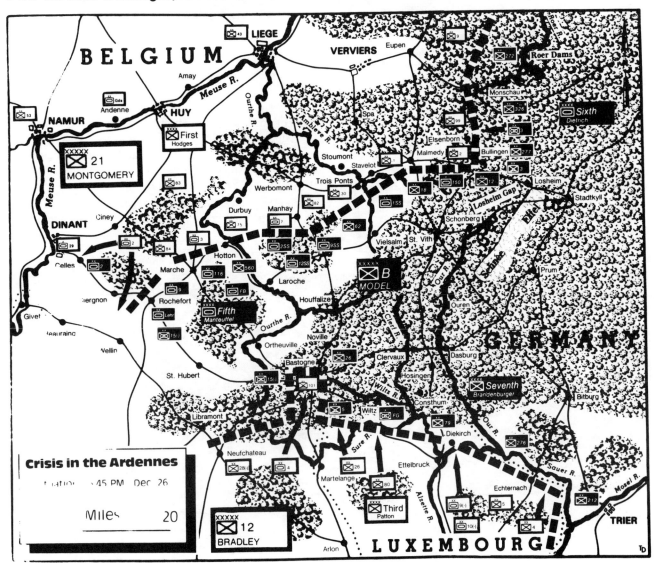

6–25. Tanks and vehicles of the 4th Armored Division advance toward Bastogne during the breakthrough. Men line the ditch at right, keeping watch over the convoys' flank.

and armor continued to advance on the town during the breakthrough (6–25 and 6–26), utilizing open territory as well as the road net.

Occasionally the incoming Americans passed a column of POWs. Those shown in 6–27 are from Oberst Ludwig Heilmann's 5. Fallschirmjäger-Division, probably captured during the fighting at Assenois. Their long, camouflaged smocks are typical of those worn by men in the German *Luftwaffe* field divisions.

Photos 6–28 and 6–29 are of American dead. They show all too clearly the cost of relieving Bastogne.

6–26. Clad in snowsuits, armored infantrymen cross a broad, snow-covered plain on 27 December, pressing ever closer to the Bastogne garrison.

6–27. Clattering past a column of POWs, an M3 half-track from the 4th Armored Division races toward Bastogne. The M3 mounts a water-cooled .30-caliber Browning machine gun.

6–28. Signal Corps photographer Pfc. D. R. Ornitz takes several well-composed, if grisly, photographs of American dead near Chaumont, Luxembourg, as Bastogne-bound half-tracks of the 4th Armored Division clatter toward their objective. Though taken from slightly different angles and locations, these photographs together provide a wide-angle view of the road.

6–29. Ornitz crosses the road, looks back, and takes a picture of another American corpse as an M3 rolls toward Bastogne. The jeep at left center was likely disabled in the Battle of Chaumont, the same action that felled the Americans nearby.

THE THREAT SUBSIDES

The sight of half-tracks and other vehicles from the 4th Armored Division parked in Bastogne's main square during 28 December (6–30) must have heartened its valiant defenders. McAuliffe had richly earned the Distinguished Service Cross, the Army's second-highest decoration, that Patton promptly pinned on him (6–31).

Although Bastogne stood relieved, the situation there was still critical. The German Army lay just outside the city and showed no sign of giving up. Thus on 29 December troops of the 101st Airborne marched out of Bastogne to fight the Germans on the city's perimeter (6–32).

Despite the fact that the Germans were still in front of and surrounded Bastogne on three sides by year's end, the arrival of support elements of the 4th Armored Division meant that cleanup and salvage activity could commence. Photo 6–33 shows such work in progress. The picture of

6–30. With Bastogne relieved, vehicles from the 4th Armored Division sit parked in its main square on 28 December.

6-31. Lieutenant General Patton chats with Brigadier General McAuliffe after awarding him the Distinguished Service Cross on 28 December. To their left is Lt. Col. Steve Chapuis, hero of the battle of Champs east of Bastogne. He, too, would soon receive the Distinguished Service Cross.

6-32. Troops of the 101st Airborne march out of Bastogne on 29 December to do battle with the Germans somewhere on the city's perimeter.

6-33. On 30 December, a 4th Armored Division tank retriever prepares to haul out a Sherman tank disabled by German shells outside Bastogne.

6–34. Burned-out buildings surround the debris-strewn main square in Bastogne on 30 December. American MPs erected a new sign warning against leaving vehicles unattended. Note the disabled M3 half-track at left.

6–35. Bombed-out citizens of Bastogne huddle together in a horse-drawn wagon, which likely also carries most of their possessions.

6–36. Guards of the 502d Parachute Infantry Regiment turn back civilians attempting to exit the Bastogne pocket northwest of the city on 30 December.

the bomb-shattered main square of Bastogne on 30 December (6–34) was taken by Pfc. Sam Gilbert, another photographer active during and after the siege. After snapping this photo, Gilbert walked one hundred feet to the left to record the street scene shown in photo 6–35. Where these Bastognians were bound on that dismal 30 December morning is open to question, as the U.S. military had cordoned off, if not completely closed, the perimeter surrounding the city. Evidently they, or a similar group, did not get far before guards from the 502d Parachute Infantry Regiment turned them back (6–36).

The end of the year found Lieutenant Colonel Chapuis's men guarding a roadblock across the highway leading to Longchamps northwest of Bastogne. Such duty on the perimeter was lonely, nerve-racking, and exceptionally dangerous.

Responding to the relief of Bastogne, the Germans attacked along the eastern and western sides of the Bastogne corridor—the *Führer-Begleit*-Brigade from the west and 1. SS-Panzer-Division from the east. Countering the German move to reseal the pocket, the 6th Armored Division moved from its position along the Saar River southwest of Diekirch, Luxembourg, into the pocket and counterattacked to the east (6–37). Attached to the 6th Armored Division were men of the 777th AAA Battalion. On this New Year's Eve, a group of these soldiers, with members

6–37. Tanks and armored infantry of the 6th Armored Division attack German troops north of Bastogne on 31 December.

6–38. Alongside members of the 101st Airborne, soldiers of the 777th AAA Battalion, which was attached to the 6th Armored Division, struggle to keep warm beside a fire on the outskirts of Bastogne on 31 December. An M3 half-track is behind them.

of the 101st Airborne, clustered around a fire for warmth (6–38).

The task of cleaning up and rebuilding started even before the Germans had been pushed away from the Bastogne pocket. Combat engineers started the New Year by clearing rubble from Bastogne's streets (6–39).

By 1 January 1945 the circumstances at Bastogne, while still serious, had settled down to the point where soldiers in the 4th Armored Division received permission to seek billeting in private residences. Thus, Cpl. Martin

Konopka went to the mayor's house in a tiny village near Bastogne and secured shelter for the squad of his half-track.

After Konopka and the others settled into their new quarters, the mayor suggested (with his daughter translating) that the men go boar hunting for a dinner perhaps more in line with their American appetites. On 2 January, the mayor accompanied his guests on their impromptu expedition. When German artillery shells crashing into the woods flushed a boar from a nearby thicket, shots rang out

6–39. Combat engineers from the 26th Armored Engineer Battalion, 6th Armored Division, begin the task of clearing rubble from Bastogne's debris-choked streets on 1 January.

from the American M1s, but the .30-caliber bullets did not seem to faze the boar. The mayor raised and fired his shotgun, laying the matter and the boar to rest (6–40). Dressing out at three hundred pounds, the animal provided Konopka's squad with quite a feast. The first dish they enjoyed was a blood pudding.

This outing was a welcome break and a much-needed touch of lightness. On the roads leading out of Bastogne were constant reminders of the bitter fighting just past and of that surely to come (6–41).

6–40. On New Year's Day, Cpl. Martin Konopka and Pvt. Charles Kelly of the 489th AAA Battalion, 4th Armored, display a wild boar as proof that they could hit their mark, albeit on a ground target. But it was the mayor's shotgun that made the kill.

6–41. A defunct convoy of derelict gasoline trucks litters the roadside on one approach to Bastogne.

CHAPTER 7

The German Offensive Slows

THE AMERICAN AIR FORCE MAKES ITSELF FELT

Inevitably, the Germans' drive westward began to run down as did their ground offensive toward the end of the first week. Reasons for their failure to press forward abounded. Apart from the Germans' own many and manifest liabilities and weaknesses—fuel shortages, poor roads, problems with supply and maintenance problems, and so on—the Americans had a deep wellspring of reserves from which to draw. Division after division was committed to the fighting in the Ardennes, and many more were available if needed. Conversely, the Germans were fighting without reserves. Virtually every division available to Generalfeldmarschall Model was already allotted to the offensive.

Nowhere was American strength more apparent than in the skies over the Ardennes. During the first days of the offensive, however, bad weather had neutralized the American advantage. The Germans knew that the cloud cover and inclement weather could not last, and when the skies cleared, the U.S. fighter-bombers would be out in droves. This occurred on 23 December for the first time since the Germans opened their offensive (7–1). In addition to air strikes, clear skies also made possible aerial reconnaissance, which gave the ground forces a far more complete view of German troop dispositions (7–2).

The frigid Belgian winter continued to cause difficulties for the ground crews of the Ninth Air Force (7–3) but not enough to keep the bombers grounded (7–4). Fighter aircraft likewise kept flying (7–5). Some destroyed Ger-

7-1. On 23 December 1944 in Manhay for the first time since the opening of the German offensive, troops of the 3d Armored Division see the contrails of Allied aircraft.

7–2. An A-20 Havoc of the 115th Photo Reconnaissance Squadron used flash and flares to take this aerial photo showing a convoy of German vehicles north of Houffalize, Belgium, on the night of 26 December.

7–3. Ninth Air Force mechanics work on a P-38 fighter at a base in Belgium. The two men at right are rigging pipes from a heater to warm up the P-38's right engine.

7–4. Bearing cheery holiday greetings for the Führer, bombs await clear weather for delivery in time for Christmas.

7-5.   P-47 Thunderbolts of the 365th Fighter Group at a Ninth Air Force base in Belgium warm up and await takeoff for missions against German armored columns. Two aircraft are taking off in the distance.

man fighters in the air (7–6); others created havoc among movements of German convoys and armor (7–7 and 7–8). In addition, accidents of a particularly irritating and dismaying kind plagued the German offensive (7–9).

The slender resources available to the *Luftwaffe* could not handle the swarms of U.S. aircraft. Even the *Luftwaffe's* New Year's Day surprise raids on Allied airfields across northern Europe (Operation *Bodenplatte,* conceived so that the German armies might continue their advance unhindered from the skies) failed to eliminate the Allied air threat. Although the operation did destroy hundreds of Allied aircraft, the losses were soon made up. Moreover, *Bodenplatte* had bled the *Luftwaffe* of its last reserves of pilots and aircraft. Ironically, the Germans' own flak shot down many as a result of poor communications. Now the *Wehrmacht* had to face the American counteroffensive without friendly air cover.

7-6.   One more FW-190 and *Luftwaffe* pilot would not be available for the final defense of the Fatherland. Maj. James Dalglish of the 354th Fighter Group scores over the Bulge.

7-7. A German ammunition truck bound for the front explodes in a blinding flash under the guns of Lt. Robert D. Law of Colorado Springs, Colorado.

7-8. Lt. Frank W. Chwateck attacks four German tanks that attempted to negotiate snow-covered roads at a Belgian crossroads on 24 December. In the center frame, Chwateck's incendiary .50-caliber bullets have just hit the lead tank.

7-9. A German Brückengerät K replacement bridge sits in the icy waters of a stream near Stavelot, Belgium, after it collapsed under the weight of a Jagdpanzer IV, which lies in the water at left. While the USAAF made invaluable contributions during the Ardennes Offensive, destroying this German replacement bridge, as claimed in the Signal Corps's caption, is not one of them.

7-10. Maj. Gen. Willard S. Paul (*right*), commanding general, 26th Infantry Division, chats with Lieutenant General Patton (*center*) and Maj. Gen. Manton Eddy (*left*) in France on 3 November 1944.

7-11. Patton and Maj. Gen. Horace L. McBride, commanding general, 80th Infantry Division, enjoy an animated discussion.

ACTION ON SOUTHERN SHOULDER OF THE BULGE

A great portion of the popular literature dealing with the Ardennes Offensive tends to focus rather narrowly on the siege of Bastogne. It is important to remember, however, that U.S. divisions on both the southern and northern shoulders of the Bulge were locked in a life-or-death struggle with the advancing German armies and by the second week of the offensive were gaining the upper hand. Two infantry divisions in particular—the 26th under Maj. Gen. Willard S. Paul (7–10) and the 80th,

commanded by Maj. Gen. Horace L. McBride (7–11)— played key roles in arresting the German tide along the southern shoulder of the Bulge.

After assembling in Luxembourg, the 80th Infantry Division, supported by the 702d Tank Battalion, attacked Merzig on 23 December. They took the town after a heavy engagement (7–12). On the following day, the division contained attacks by the Germans at Heiderscheid and Ettelbrück, Luxembourg, and advanced to the Saar.

At Heiderscheid, an American photographer took three photographs of damaged German armor (7–13, 7–14 and 7–15), giving some idea of the fierce action

7-12. Humbled *Grenadiere* from the 914. Grenadier-Regiment, 352. Volksgrenadier-Division, line up in front of their captors near Merzig, Luxembourg, on 24 December, after their battle with the U.S. 319th Infantry Regiment, 80th Infantry Division.

7-13. The day after Christmas, American soldiers from the 702d Tank Battalion inspect a PzKfpw V Panther heavy tank from the *Führer-Grenadier*-Brigade. It was knocked out during heavy fighting at Heiderscheid, Luxembourg. Photographer H. Miller, possibly a German armor enthusiast, took this and the following two photographs.

7-14. Curious Americans in Heiderscheid inspect a Sturmgeschütz IV that was abandoned by the *Führer-Grenadier*-Brigade. One man sits atop, one peers down the muzzle, and a third, Lt. L. M. Barrington, peeps into the driver's compartment.

7-15. Another Sturmgeschütz and a wrecked SdKfz 251 half-track stand on the outskirts of Heiderscheid. The torn body of a *Führer-Grenadier* lies close by at right.

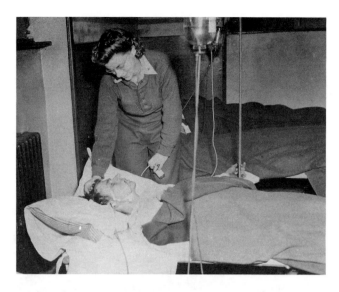

7–16. POW Emil Gronen, likely from the *Führer-Grenadier*-Brigade, receives medical attention from army nurse Lillian Wilson in the 60th Field Hospital in Heiderscheid.

in this sector. In contrast, photo 7–16 shows U.S. Army nurse Lillian Wilson giving medical care to a German POW.

The 26th Infantry Division also assembled in Luxembourg, where it was committed behind the 80th Infantry Division. Clearing Eschdorf by 26 December, it then pushed forward to the Wiltz River. Photo 7–17, taken during a hiatus in the heavy fighting, gives an excellent picture of a mortar crew from the 26th Division's 101st Infantry Regiment in action.

After capturing Haller, Luxembourg, on Christmas Day, the 5th Infantry Division gradually reduced the Ger-

man flanks during the last week in December. It did so in tandem with the 4th Infantry Division, lately engaged in the reduction of Echternach. Action on the southern shoulder prior to the U.S. counteroffensive in January is portrayed in 7–18, wherein infantrymen of the 11th Regiment, 5th Infantry Division, approach German positions near Haller. At the same location, men of the 19th Field Artillery Battalion stand equally ready as they prepare to shell German lines (7–19).

At Echternach, a photographer captured this unhappy image of German casualties from 26 December (7–20). The 4th Division would capture the town the next day.

7–17. An 81mm mortar crew from the 101st Infantry Regiment, 26th Infantry Division, hurls mortar rounds at German positions near Bavigne, Luxembourg, on New Year's Eve. Soldiers with ready rounds in hand stand by at right and left, while a private first class at far right communicates with a spotter. The man standing guard at the rear with an M1 carbine illustrates how that lighter weapon was typically used.

7-18. On 1 January infantrymen in snowsuits from the 11th Regiment, 5th Infantry Division, press German positions in the Bulge's southern sector near Haller, Luxembourg.

7-19. A 105mm howitzer from the 19th Field Artillery Battalion, 5th Infantry Division, stands ready in a well-dug-in and camouflaged position near Haller. The smokestack rising through the last camouflage net at left likely provides the barest minimum of creature comforts to the gun crew.

7-20. German casualties of the 212. Volksgrenadier-Division on frozen fields south of Echternach on 26 December.

7–21. Advancing over frigid snow-covered hills near Bettange, troops of the 35th Division advance against the 5. Fallschirmjäger-Division and elements of the 15. Panzergrenadier-Division on 28 December.

Quite close to Bettange troops from the 35th Infantry Division were committed to action in the Bulge (7–21).

Like so many other divisions that went into the fight on the southern shoulder, the 35th Infantry Division under Maj. Gen. Paul W. Baade (7–22) assembled at Arlon before crossing the Sûre. It fell in behind the 4th Armored Division, which was on its way to Bastogne.

Photo 7–23 shows men from the 345th Infantry Regiment of Maj. Gen. Frank L. Culin's (7–24) 87th Infantry Division advance through Moircy, west of the Bastogne pocket, on 31 December. Just the day before the 345th Infantry had taken Moircy, only to lose the village to a German counterattack the next day. In a seesaw battle, the Americans secured Moircy for good on 1 January.

Resting in defensive positions along the Roer prior to the offensive, the 2d Armored Division was committed to the Ardennes fighting near the tip of the Bulge salient. It went into position near Marche, Belgium, on 22 December, engaging the 9. Panzer-Division. Over the next week the 2d Armored cleared Celles and Humain (7–25 and 7–26) and was relieved by the 83d Division.

7–22. Maj. Gen. Paul W. Baade, commanding general, 35th Infantry Division.

7–23. On 31 December, men from the 345th Infantry Regiment, 87th Infantry Division, in Moircy, southeast of St. Hubert, Belgium.

7-24. Maj. Gen. Frank L. Culin, commanding general, 87th Infantry Division.

7-25. Humain, Belgium, on 28 December. A U.S. 76mm antitank gun lies knocked out, a victim in the battle for Humain.

7-26. Three Panthers from Generalmajor von Elverfeld's 9. Panzer-Division, destroyed by the U.S. 2d Armored Division, rest in silent formation near Humain.

Photo 7–27 shows Pvt. Riley Tillman, one of "those damned engineers." He stands ready to elicit further German curses by blowing up a bridge near Marche.

In response to the German offensive, the 84th Division moved into the Marche vicinity. It set up a defense perimeter there during 21 and 22 December and went into action between Hargimont and Rochefort in the sleet and snow. On the defensive until 27 December, it remained engaged, gradually pushing back the German pocket (7–28), until the American counteroffensive on 3 January.

Additional evidence of increasing German misfortune took the form of a destroyed Panther tank (7–29), a sight that would not have evoked any sympathy from the townspeople of Stavelot (7–30). SS troops murdered twenty-three civilians in Stavelot because a single American rifleman opened fire from the Legaye house during the Germans' capture of the town (7–31). A war crimes trial held in Liège ended on 31 July 1948 with the conviction of Gustav Knittel's freckle-faced staff company commander, Obersturmführer Heinrich Goltz, and eight others for complicity in the crime (see photo 4–48).

7-27. Pvt. Riley Tillman stands ready to ply his trade of blowing up bridges near Marche, Belgium, in the event of a German breakthrough during 30 December. Tillman was a member of the 1st Combat Engineer Battalion, assigned to the 84th Infantry Division.

7-28. On 30 December, a camouflaged M10 tank destroyer assigned to the 84th Infantry Division lies in wait for unsuspecting German tanks from the 116. Panzer-Division in Hotton, Belgium.

7-29. Knocked out by units of the 75th Division, a Panther from *Hitlerjugend* sits at the Belgian crossroads of Grandmenil on 30 December.

7-30. The battered town of Stavelot in the Amblève River valley as seen from the positions of the 30th Infantry Division and looking east across the river to those of the 18. Volksgrenadier-Division on the bluffs beyond, on 30 December.

7-31. Last rites for the victims of German atrocities in Stavelot. Massacre victims would be buried in a common grave on 30 December.

II. SS-PANZERKORPS'S DRIVE BLUNTED AT MANHAY

While SS-Gruppenführer Priess's I. SS-Panzerkorps was stalemated in the north, SS-Obergruppenführer Bittrich's II. SS-Panzerkorps, comprised of the 2. and 9. SS-Panzer-divisions, slipped off to the south and west toward two key crossroads—Baraque de Fraiture and Manhay. Advancing side by side with *Das Reich* on the left and *Hohenstaufen* on the right, Bittrich's Panzerkorps captured Baraque de Fraiture on Christmas Eve after a sharp fight. After reorganizing, they moved on Manhay (7–32) and the area northeast of that town the same night.

Meeting the German attacks was the 7th Armored Division, only just withdrawn from St. Vith. The 7th Armored set up defenses in Manhay proper. The 3d Armored Division girded its right flank; the 9th Armored CCB, its left. Farther north and east, Maj. Gen. James A. Gavin's (7–33) 82d Airborne Division bore the brunt of the attack by the 9. SS-Panzer-Division under Sturmbannführer Eberhard Telkamp (7–34). In bitter fighting that marked

7-32. **Sturmbannführer Ernst Krag, SS-Aufklärungs-Abteilung 2, 2. SS-Panzer-Division. His *Kampfgruppe* led the way to Manhay.**

7-34. **Sturmbannführer Eberhard Telkamp, SS-Panzer-Regiment 9, 9. SS-Panzer-Division. His tanks would spearhead the attack against the U.S. 82d Airborne Division.**

7-33. **Maj. Gen. James A. Gavin, commanding general, 82d Airborne Division. His division would anchor the Americans' left flank against Bittrich's attack.**

7-35. **Waiting for German armor to come clattering down the road, a 3d Armored Division soldier guards the approaches to Manhay with his rocket launcher on 23 December. He would have only one day to wait.**

7-36. Tanks of the 116. Panzer-Division—PzKpfw IV "611" at left and a Panther at right—undergo scrutiny by men of the 3d Armored Division at Hotton on 26 December, three days after turning back a German attack on the town.

the deepest penetration of the II. SS-Panzerkorps, Manhay was lost on Christmas Eve (7–35). It was recaptured when the Americans counterattacked on 27 December.

Although it held the 116. Panzer in check at Hotton (7–36), the 3d Armored Division lost control of a vital crossroads southeast of Manhay. This partially cleared the way for the II. SS-Panzerkorps's advance.

Photos 7–37, 7–38, and 7–39 portray two German POWs. One looks definitely uneasy, perhaps uncertain as to what treatment awaited him. The other has donned a stoical expression. In his caption, the photographer presumed to describe the soldier—hardly the German ideal blond, blue-eyed Aryan—as a "hardened, ruthless killer." Perhaps he was; perhaps he wasn't!

7-37. A young SS private, probably from *Das Reich,* undergoes interrogation in Manhay on 23 December, one day before his comrades "liberated" the town, albeit temporarily.

7-38. With tousled hair and a head injury, the infantryman casts a troubled, uncertain stare at photographer Lt. T. S. Noble.

7-39. Another SS *Grenadier,* this one a Sturmmann, seems somewhat indifferent to Noble.

7–40. Manhay after the Americans recaptured it, shown on 30 December.

Manhay was destroyed by violence, an action repeated countless times during the war all over Europe. Only the prospect of ridding the world of such a regime as Hitler's could have justified this continued evisceration of Europe's cities, villages, and towns (7–40). Did the citizens of Manhay regard the Americans as liberators or just more destroyers (7–41)?

7–41. Pvt. Clarence Severtsgaar scans the horizon from the turret of his M36 tank destroyer near Manhay on 27 December. The photo shows clearly the open-top turret common to all U.S. tank destroyers. Ration boxes are strewn around the dug-in position. From the shadows and the bright sunlight, it is apparent that the tank destroyer has set up on the edge of the woods.

CHAPTER 8

The Allies Crush the Bulge

In the beginning, the Americans had been strangely blind to, or incredulous of, German troop movements opposite the Ardennes, and even after the offensive started, many labeled it only a spoiling expedition. Now, they seemed equally reluctant to believe that the threat was waning. Eisenhower wanted to raise some European divisions, and he asked the Joint Chiefs of Staff to speed up the sailing of reinforcements.

With Ike's approval, Winston Churchill wrote to Joseph Stalin and asked if they could count on a major Russian offensive during January. This was a prime mistake. Later Stalin would claim that his offensive, which began on 12 January, had broken "the German attack in the West," and he would use it in pressing his demands at Yalta. Actually the Russian offensive had nothing to do

with the Battle of the Bulge; by that time the Allies' victory was no longer in doubt. On 3 January Hitler had conceded that the plan had failed and on 8 January ordered limited withdrawal.

ACTION ON THE SOUTHERN SHOULDER

The fighting did not cease, however; the Germans contested the Allies at every step. Bastogne and its vicinity, in particular, continued to see bitter action. Photo 8–1, taken early in January 1945, shows two GIs guarding against German infiltration on the eve of the U.S. counteroffen-

8–1. In a wooded area near the Bastogne corridor in the early days of January 1945, Pvts. John P. MacFarlane and Loyd W. Lockwood of the 35th Infantry Division man a .30-caliber Browning machine gun.

sive at Bastogne. After that action commenced, the U.S. 30th Infantry Division took Villers-la-Bonne-Eau on 10 January. Fighting house to house, elements of the division took Oubourcy and Lutrebois. Then it withdrew to Metz for some well-earned rest and rehabilitation, leaving behind many enemy casualties (8–2).

Meanwhile, the 11th Armored Division was moving toward the Bastogne corridor. Reaching Jodenville, some four miles southwest of Bastogne, the troops paused for a meal and a brief rest (8–3).

Each engagement resulted in the capture of at least a few German POWs, such as the two forlorn youngsters from the 12. SS-Panzer-Division shown in photo 8–4. They were captured at Margaret, Belgium, three miles east of Bastogne. Their obvious youth suggests they were conscripts from the *Hitlerjugend*. While prisoners such as these boys—little more than children—were pitiable, the Allies treated all POWs the same and incarcerated them in stockades. Also taken during the 6th Armored Division's brief hold on Margaret on 7 January were older soldiers from the 12. SS-Panzer Division (8–5).

The 6th Armored Division became heavily engaged in the Wardin-Margaret sector east of Bastogne on New Year's Eve. Heavy German attacks forced the 6th Armored's withdrawal, but the division later counterattacked. It finally cleared Wardin on 12 January and Margaret two days later.

Following a series of failed attacks near the Wiltz River, the 26th Infantry Division regrouped and suc-

8–2. The lonely grave of an anonymous German paratrooper of the 5. Fallschirmjäger-Division lies in the woods east of Bastogne in a sector that the U.S. 30th Division retook. Note the paratrooper's helmet, his Mauser rifle, and the crude wooden cross.

ceeded in establishing a bridgehead on the river on 10 January. It captured the town of Wiltz, Luxembourg, on 22 January. Four miles to the south of Wiltz on 10 January, two men of the 26th Infantry had time to savor welcome if outdated Sunday comics from the 17 September 1944 issue of the Harrisburg (Pa.) *Telegraph* (8–6).

8–3. In position with the 11th Armored Division, troops relax after a meal in a barn near Jodenville, Belgium. One soldier (*center*) appears to be writing a letter home.

8–4. Taken prisoner by the 50th Armored Infantry Battalion of the 6th Armored Division in Magaret, two young men from the 12. SS-Panzer-Division cast vacuous glances at their captors. Note that the *Grenadier* at right has tucked his tunic into trousers held up by a knotted cord in lieu of a belt.

8–5. An American soldier searches members of the 12. SS-Panzer-Division. The Sturmmann (*center*) wears the *Hitlerjugend* divisional cuff title on his tunic. His SS sleeve eagle has been removed, perhaps by an American souvenir hunter.

8–6. Pvt. Forrest Parker and Sgt. Elmar Hurar indulge in the much-welcomed mindless diversion of the Sunday comics in the 26th Infantry's sector at Goesdorf, four miles south of Wiltz, Luxembourg. A .30-caliber machine gun is in position behind the two soldiers. In the *Dick Tracy* panel facing the camera, Tracy rushes into Gravel Gertie's shack in search of "The Brow."

8-7. An M10 tank destroyer of the 712th Tank Battalion, 90th Infantry Division, advances past the snow-covered ruins of Berle, Luxembourg, on 12 January.

After pre-Bulge fighting against the Germans' West Wall defenses, the 90th Infantry Division rested on the west bank of the Saar. It went on the attack again on 9 January. It captured Bras on 13 January and attacked across the Clerf River ten days later (8–7). The establishment of two bridgeheads across the Our River on 29 January brought the unit's activity in the Ardennes campaign to a close.

Even though Wiltz had not yet been recaptured, by 14 January graves registration personnel from the 26th Infantry Division were collecting the bodies of both American and German dead (8–8). The 26th Infantry and the 6th Cavalry Group recaptured Wiltz on 22 January (8–9). That day it became evident that the Germans' own grave registration details had been busy at Wiltz (8–10). These German dead were buried in front of the town's police station at right. The majority of German dead were disinterred and laid to rest in larger cemeteries in the decade following the war.

The Americans continued to take prisoners. Not all the Germans captured were combat personnel, however. The medic shown in photo 8–11 was taken near Butgenbach

8-8. On 14 January, graves registration personnel from the 26th Infantry Division collect both American and German dead in the aftermath of fighting near Wiltz, Luxembourg. Note the chains on the rear tires of the jeep.

8-9. An aerial view of Wiltz on 22 January after its recapture by the 26th Infantry Division and the 6th Cavalry Group.

8-10. German graves in Wiltz on 22 January. A victim's helmet rests atop one of the crosses.

8-11. Americans detain a captured German medic. Clad in a red-crossed overlay and helmet cover, he carries his supplies in two U.S. field glass cases.

8-12. Two German Opel trucks are upended along a roadside near Marbourg, Luxembourg on 31 January. The second truck is at left, back in the fog. Note the first truck's *Wehrmacht-Heer* license plate, identifiable by its "WH-" prefix.

on 24 January. And of course the Germans lost matériel as well as men. Pictured in photo 8–12 are two Opel trucks, victims of U.S. air attacks.

As the Americans entered villages previously occupied by the Germans, the Nazi penchant for grandiloquent slogans became evident. The words "Ein Volk! Ein Reich! Ein Führer!" [One people! One nation! One leader!] fail to impress the GI who prepares to eat lunch beneath the motto (8–13). At Troisvierges, Luxembourg, the Germans promised the natives—or themselves—what translates as

"Behind the last battle of this war stands our victory" (8–14).

At Clervaux, Luxembourg, the Americans came across evidence that the Germans were literally running out of gas; they found a spanking new, unharmed Panther tank. Its crew had tried to blow it up, but the charge failed to detonate (8–15). Even more symbolic of the turn in German fortunes is the pathetic military cemetery at Clervaux, soaking in a February thaw (8–16).

8-13. Pvt. Joseph Klem of the 357th Infantry Regiment, 90th Infantry Division, prepares to munch on his noonday ration at Binsfeld, Luxembourg.

8-14. On 6 February, Signal Corps photographer Tech/4 Aaron Lubitsch pauses alongside a building bearing a German slogan in Troisvierges, Luxembourg, about eight miles due east of Houffalize, Belgium.

8-15. In Clervaux, Luxembourg, a brand-new Panther tank sits intact, out of
gas, and with the turret hatch open.

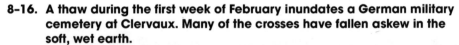

8-16. A thaw during the first week of February inundates a German military
cemetery at Clervaux. Many of the crosses have fallen askew in the
soft, wet earth.

8–17. A Sherman tank of the 2d Armored Division passes a snow-covered PzKpfw V Panther in a roadside ditch near Grandmenil, Belgium.

ACTION ON THE NORTHERN SHOULDER

Somewhat similar scenes were occurring on the Bulge's northern shoulder. Here the Americans found another abandoned Panther (8–17) and took more POWs (8–18 and 8–19).

On 3 January, the 3d Armored attacked toward Hauffalize and fought its way to Provedroux by 8 January.

The day before, some of its tanks were held up temporarily by an abandoned German tank (8–20). Under its commander, Maj. Gen. Maurice Rose (8–21), the 3d Armored proceeded on its way, reaching the Ourthe River by 19 January.

After taking Steinbach during the U.S. counteroffensive, the 1st Infantry Division, led by Brig. Gen. Clift Andrus (8–22), opened the way for the 7th Armored Division's drive to recapture St. Vith. The 1st Infantry

8–18. German army POWs line up with *Soldbücher* in hand after the 82d Airborne Division captured them near Basse-Bodeux, Belgium on 3 January, just as the U.S. counteroffensive got under way. The soldier in the front of the line wears an Army decal on his helmet.

8-19. This young infantryman, another prisoner captured by the 82d Airborne near Fosse on 4 January, wears a snowsuit with a waist belt and 7.92mm ammunition pouches.

8-20. Sherman tanks from the 3d Armored Division pause in their advance along the northern edge of the Bulge in the Manhay-Houffalize sector near Baraque de Fraiture on 7 January and wait for a German tank to be cleared from the road ahead.

8-21. Maj. Gen. Maurice Rose, in command of the 3d Armored Division.

8-22. Brig. Gen. Clift Andrus, commanding general, 1st Infantry Division.

8-23. **Captured by 1st Division soldiers during the fighting near Steinbach, a *Luftwaffe* Obergefreiter from the 3. Fallschirmjäger-Division glares at Signal Corps photographer Sgt. Bill Augustine in Weywertz, Belgium on 15 January.**

8-24. **Another Obergefreiter is far less appreciative of Augustine's photographic efforts, shielding his face from the camera. An Unteroffizier stands in the background at right.**

8-25. **An SS private surrenders to the 3d Armored Division. The *Grenadier* wears a familiar complement of uniform parts—service tunic, camouflage smock, and greatcoat.**

took its share of prisoners, such as the Obergefreiter glaring angrily at the photographer in photo 8–23. His fellow paratrooper hides his face in photo 8–24. He probably feels keenly the disgrace of capture, because, unlike many of the misfits in his division, this man is a full-fledged paratrooper who has earned the coveted *Fallschirm-jägerabzeichen,* or *Luftwaffe* paratrooper badge, and wears a ribbon for the Iron Cross 2d class on the breast of his *Fliegerbluse.* To the left of the paratrooper badge is a *DRL* sports badge. At right is a *Hitlerjugend* proficiency badge, evidence of the German practice of channeling its better young men into the SS and *Fallschirmjäger* formations. On its drive toward the Ourthe River on 15 January, the 3d Armored also bagged the SS private shown in photo 8–25.

The 101st Airborne Division maintained its position in the Bastogne defenses until 9 January, when elements took up the advance. While the 506th Parachute Infantry moved on Foy (8–26), a sister regiment, the 502d Infantry, captured Rachamps on 16 January. After fighting its way north and east of Bastogne, the 101st went into a defensive position on the Moder River.

Inevitably, the retreating Germans planted mines in the roads in front of the advancing American divisions. Both sides used exploders (8–27) to clear the roads. Such vehicles, with their large metal wheels and thick undercarriages, were practically invulnerable to mines.

8–26. Foy, Belgium, just after the arrival of elements of the 506th Parachute Infantry, 101st Airborne, on 16 January. Horses have strayed into the road at right. An ambulance from the medical unit is parked beside the horses' water trough at left.

8–27. Four miles east of Malmédy near Faymonville on 16 January, a T1E1 mine exploder works to clear the road of mines, while an M3 half-track gingerly follows close behind.

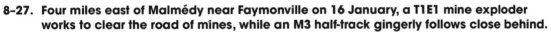

8–28. Army photographer Garrell approaches the town of Houffalize, Belgium, from the west on 18 January.

The 2d Armored Division liberated Houffalize on 16 January. Two days later, a Signal Corps photographer arrived (8–28) and rode down the shattered main street (8–29).

Meanwhile, the 7th Armored pressed on over the snow-covered roads (8–30), moving through Born in house-to-house fighting on 21 January and Hunnigen on 22 January. It ultimately cleared St. Vith on 23 January.

Air liaison officers from the Ninth Air Force were naturally interested to see the results of their air strikes. They took time out to look over one of the many tanks and vehicles that had fallen victim to the American fliers and to the 7th Armored (8–31).

8–29. Garrell rides down the main road into shell-torn Houffalize. The sign board warns advancing soldiers that the road ahead is unmarked.

**8-30. Racing over snow-covered roads, tanks of the 7th Armored Division
push on toward St. Vith.**

**8-31. Air liaison officers of the Ninth Air Force—(*left to right*) Maj. Albert Triers, Maj.
William Abbot Jr., and 1st Lt. Richard Zinkowski—inspect a PzKpfw V, one of many
tanks and other vehicles that the IX Tactical Air Command and the advancing
7th Armored Division had destroyed. The Panther seems to be parked in front of
Hôtel des Ardennes, as if would-be German guests had stopped to check in.**

8–32. Soldiers of the 7th Armored Division guard three German officers captured on the way into St. Vith. The officers at left are rather neatly attired and relatively well turned out, while the man at right appears somewhat disheveled, wearing a crumpled, dirty snowsuit.

Among the first prisoners the 7th Armored took during the push into St. Vith were the three officers shown in photo 8–32. When the 7th Armored entered St. Vith—or what was left of it—a certain uneasiness still prevailed, as reflected in the wary, upward gaze of the riflemen in photo 8–33.

The men of the 75th Infantry Division were newcomers to the Bulge. This campaign was their first action after landing at Le Havre on 13 December. After occupying defensive positions on the Ourthe River, the division moved in heavy fighting to Grandmenil on 5 January and attacked across the Salm River on 15 January. Photo 8–34 shows the division near St. Vith on 23 January. It had just cleared Grand Bois the day before and would capture Aldringen on 25 January.

The various armored pieces that the Germans had to abandon were of more than "souvenir" interest or objects of curiosity. For example, the Flakpanzer IV from *Kampfgruppe* Peiper discovered near Buchholtz was well preserved enough that it was shipped to the United States for evaluation and testing (8–35).

8–33. Snowsuit-clad members of a rifle squad (possibly assigned to the Sherman tank in the background) from the 7th Armored Division warily observe the windows above them in the debris-strewn streets of St. Vith on 23 January. The wall at left appears ready to topple onto the men below.

8–34. Advancing through heavy snow and incoming German shellfire, infantrymen of the 75th Division move forward near St. Vith on 23 January.

8–35. On 27 January, American troops pass a PzKpfw IV-chassised Flakpanzer *Wirbelwind* that was abandoned by *Kampfgruppe* Peiper near Buchholtz during the first days of the offensive.

8-36. Men of the 325th Glider Infantry, 82d Airborne Division, commit themselves to the final advance on Herresbach on 28 January, the date of the village's liberation. The men drag a heavily laden ammunition sled through the snow. While some have on snowsuits, others do not.

The following series of photos convey more than most the brutally cold and inclement weather the soldiers endured in pressing back against the German Bulge in January 1945. The bitter cold and biting winds were recurrent themes in the letters sent home by Chaplain Arthur D. Wenger of the 76th Infantry Division, just coming into line during this period south of Echternach.

Photos 8–36, 8–37, and 8–38 depict troops of the 82d Airborne. Although quite similar in content and composition, they were taken near Herresbach by three different photographers accompanying the division on the same day. Another snow scene of a different nature underlines the suffering that war inflicted upon the most innocent and peaceful people and places (8–39).

8-37. A Sherman tank of the 740th Tank Battalion, attached to the 82d Airborne only the week before, crunches through heavy snow near Herresbach.

8–38. Soldiers trudge one behind the other in boot-deep snow just prior to the fall of Herresbach on 29 January.

8–39. Snow drifts over the pews and floor of a shattered church in Krinkelt, Belgium, on 1 February, retaken earlier by the 2d Infantry Division.

8–40. On 3 January, machine gunners of the 104th Infantry, 4th Armored Division, cover an advancing tank in the Bastogne corridor. Note the photographer's shadow at right, cast by the early morning light.

ACTIVITY IN OR NEAR THE BULGE POCKET

Even though the Americans were pushing back the Bulge (8–40), the Bastogne area was still a thoroughly dangerous place. Photo 8–41 shows an ambulance that a German artillery shell put out of action around 9 January. Fortunately, all of the litter bearers escaped injury.

On 13 January northeast of Bastogne, infantry and vehicles of the 6th Armored Division advanced against the Germans—probably Generalleutnant Hans-Kurt Höcker's 167. Volksgrenadier (8–42). Five days later, Maj. Gen. Maxwell D. Taylor turned control of Bastogne over to Major General Middleton of the VIII Corps (8–43). Middleton gave General Taylor (8–44) a receipt for Bastogne (8–45).

8–41. An ambulance of the 501st Medical Battalion, 101st Airborne Division, lies wrecked near the outskirts of Bastogne, another victim of a German artillery shell about 9 January.

8-42. Aerial photo of the village of Bizory, northeast of Bastogne, as the U.S. 6th Armored Division advances. Note the telltale tank tracks in the snow.

8-43. Maj. Gen. Maxwell D. Taylor turns over control of Bastogne to VIII Corps commander Major General Middleton on 18 January. An MP sergeant with a camera stands at left.

8-44. Major General Taylor, commanding general, 101st Airborne Division.

8-45. Maxwell Taylor's receipt for Bastogne—battered but serviceable and "disinfected."

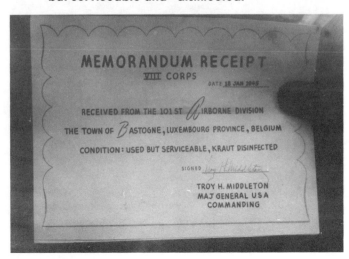

MEMORANDUM RECEIPT
VIII CORPS
DATE 18 JAN 1945

RECEIVED FROM THE 101ST AIRBORNE DIVISION
THE TOWN OF BASTOGNE, LUXEMBOURG PROVINCE, BELGIUM
CONDITION: USED BUT SERVICEABLE, KRAUT DISINFECTED
SIGNED

TROY H. MIDDLETON
MAJ GENERAL USA
COMMANDING

8–46. Upended vehicles of Team Cherry, wrecked during the siege of Bastogne, have been pushed into a ditch on the road to Longvilly northeast of the city.

8–47. Supply convoy of the 90th Infantry Division rolls through the streets of Bastogne on 22 January. This picture, taken by Sgt. C. F. Anders, is perhaps the photograph most frequently associated with Bastogne and the Battle of the Bulge.

In the aftermath of the fighting at Bastogne, one can see wrecked vehicles northeast of the city (8–46) and a supply convoy rolling through its streets (8–47).

HOSPITALS

The most destructive war in the history of humankind visited suffering on one American at a highly painful and personal level. Before entering surgery for his multiple wounds, he received transfusions of whole blood (8–48).

At this time field hospital conditions were quite primitive (8–49), and of course they served a steady stream of patients. In one peak sixty-three-hour period, the 51st Field Hospital near Aisne, Belgium, cleared over one thousand patients (8–50). Despite all that skill and dedication could do, they could not save all the wounded. Each hospital, therefore, had its complement of chaplains to deal with the inevitable and to give the dying what comfort they could (8–51).

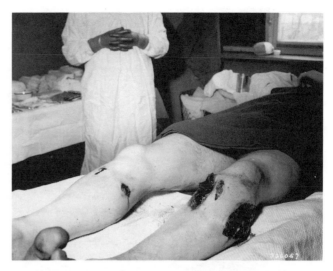

8–48. A soldier suffering compound fractures in both legs from gunshot and shrapnel wounds awaits the attention of surgeons in the 111th Evacuation Hospital in Luxembourg.

8–49. Army medical personnel of the 51st Field Hospital operate in primitive conditions near Aisne, Belgium. They are (*left to right*) Tech/4 James Polite, Lt. Helen Johnson, and Capt. I. R. Hayman. Gas bottles and anesthesia equipment sit in the foreground.

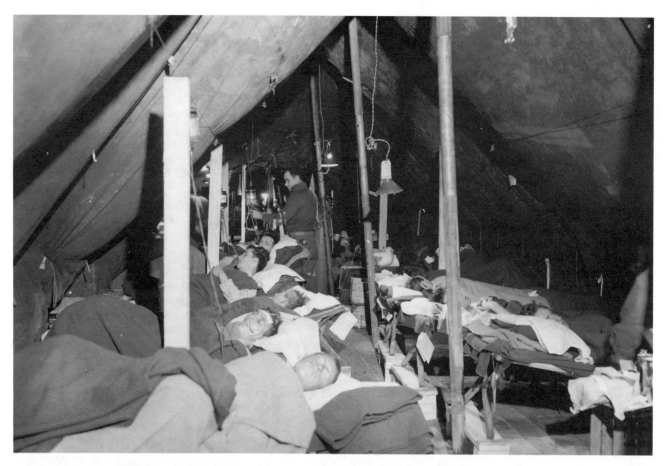

8-50. Battle casualties from the Bulge crowd a post-operative tent near Aisne. The pyramidal tent offers shelter to patients for whom quarters are not yet available.

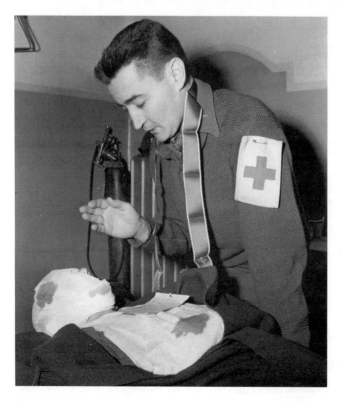

8-51. At a medical clearing station near Ettelbruck, Luxembourg, a Catholic chaplain from the 5th Infantry Division—Maj. Harold O. Prudell—administers last rites on 29 January to a soldier who was seriously wounded along the Bulge's southern shoulder.

CHAPTER 9

Aftermath

MALMÉDY (BAUGNEZ)—THE INVESTIGATION AND TRIAL

The legal and investigative processes culminating in the Malmédy trial commenced shortly after the massacre at Baugnez. The Supreme Headquarters, Allied Expedition-ary Force's (SHAEF) Standing Court began assembling available evidence and relatively early established that *Kampfgruppe* Peiper was responsible for the killings. By June 1945, the task of rounding up the *Kampfgruppe's* surviving members began in earnest, although the searches yielded fruit very slowly (9–1). Meanwhile, the

9–1. In a POW stockade near Passau, Germany, on 7 May 1945, battered German soldiers stand in line after being identified as suspects in the Baugnez massacre. None of the men here, however, match known photos of any defendants in the Malmédy trial. Their presence in *Kampfgruppe* Peiper would be surprising in any case, as most seem to be decidedly middle-aged.

9-2. The flag-draped Malmédy Massacre Memorial at Baugnez, Belgium—seen here on 27 July 1945—was a temporary structure, molded out of concrete.

U.S. Army wasted no time in erecting a memorial at Baugnez to the victims. It was one of the first set in place in Europe (9–2).

In the chaos following the war, it took some time to determine the whereabouts of the principals in the case. In August, Peiper was discovered in a POW cage north of Munich near Freising. During the remainder of 1945 and 1946, investigators continued to compile evidence, bring in and identify members of the *Kampfgruppe,* interrogate them, and secure sworn statements under various degrees of intimidation and duress. By the spring of 1946, as the trial loomed near, the weight of evidence against *Kampfgruppe* Peiper was overwhelming.

In addition to Peiper and his men, three generals above them in the chain of command would stand trial: Oberst-gruppenführer Josef "Sepp" Dietrich of the 6. Panzer-Armee, Gruppenführer Hermann Priess of the I. SS-Panzerkorps, and Oberführer Fritz Krämer. Although believed to have survived the war, Oberführer Wilhelm Mohnke, the commander of the 1. SS-Panzer-Division, actually had committed suicide.

Witnesses for the prosecution likewise also had to be rounded up for the upcoming Malmédy trial, which would be held during May and June 1946. The testimony of the following survivors, who flew back from the United States to participate, would be particularly interesting (9–3). As the senior surviving American at Baugnez, Virgil P. Lary, of late a student at the University of Kentucky, was a star witness. Carl R. Daub had persuaded Lary to abandon any further resistance and to surrender to the SS

9-3. On 9 April 1946, six of the massacre's survivors gather in front of the concrete monument (*left to right*): Virgil P. Lary, Kenneth Ahrens, Homer D. Ford, Carl R. Daub, Kenneth E. Kingston, and Samuel Dobyns.

troops. Kenneth E. Kingston was with Lary when a German officer apprehended the pair and demanded that some of the captured Americans be detailed to drive away the newly captured vehicles for the *Kampfgruppe.* Samuel Dobyns was an ambulance driver from the 99th Infantry who happened to be accompanying the convoy, and Homer D. Ford was the MP stationed at Madame Bodarwé's café. As for Kenneth Ahrens, he had survived at Malmédy because his uniform was so soaked with blood the Germans left him for dead.

Opening at Dachau (9–4 and 9–5)—one can hardly fail to note the grim irony—at 1000 on 16 May 1946, the trial was commonly known as the Malmédy massacre trial, although its official title was *U.S. vs. Valentin Bersin, et al.* Defendant Bersin was unfortunate enough to head the alphabetized list of defendants. Although the trial was to establish an accounting of responsibility only for the Baugnez incident, evidence was presented relating to other depredations of the *Waffen-SS,* such as the atrocities committed at Honsfeld, Stavelot, and other locations.

The defendants were no longer considered prisoners of war. Instead they were now civilian internees, or accused war criminals, and accordingly lost certain protections that the Geneva Convention of 1929 had provided for prisoners of war. A General Military Government Court would try them. All of the defendants faced both a general charge and individual charges in a bill of particulars.

The judges had extreme latitude in determining what evidence could be accepted or excluded from the proceedings. A verdict would require two-thirds of the bench.

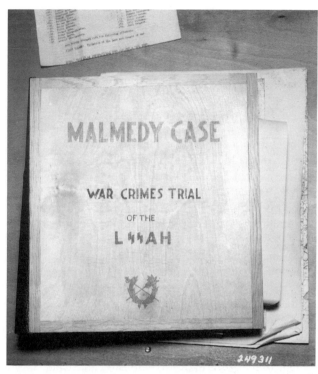

9–4. The cover of the book containing the charges and evidence for the Malmédy trial. Note the typed list of defendants immediately above.

9–5. The building at Dachau where the General Military Government Court convened on 16 July, the day sentences for seventy-three of the defendants were announced.

Brig. Gen. Josiah T. Dabney of the 3d Infantry Division was the presiding officer of the court. The law member was Col. Abraham H. Rosenfeld. Line officers, all colonels, occupied the other six positions on the court. The trial judge advocate was Lt. Col. Burton F. Ellis; chief defense counsel was Col. Willis M. Everett Jr. (9–6)

The trial began on 16 May 1946 with another ironic twist: The defendants, assigned numbers in alphabetical order, suffered the same impersonal anonymity as the corpses of the Malmédy massacre. Photo 9–7 shows that the left end of the prisoners' dock was weighed down heavily with officers. Immediately behind Dietrich and to the left is Gustav Knittel. Left of Knittel is former Hauptsturmführer Oskar Klingelhöfer, who was commander of the 7. SS-Panzer-Regiment 1. It was the lead company of Sturmannführer Werner Pötschke's I. Abteilung, which was directly responsible for initiating the massacre. To Dietrich's right on the first row are Krämer and Priess (caught by surprise while pulling at his nose). The MP at left guards the officers while the enlisted men and NCOs are segregated on the right end of the dock (9–8). The members of the court are seated at far right.

One of the trial's dramatic moments came when Virgil Lary identified George Fleps (assistant gunner in *Panzer IV* "731," commanded by Hauptscharführer Hans Siptrott) as the individual who fired the first shots into the surrendered American soldiers at Baugnez (9–9). Lary testified that, after the machine-gun fire started, the German soldiers laughed maniacally and seemed very much to enjoy the scene.

9–6. The trial's antagonists—Col. Willis M. Everett Jr., chief defense counsel, and Lt. Col. Burton F. Ellis, trial judge advocate—in animated conversation during a court recess on 26 June 1946.

9–7. Former 6. Panzer-Armee commander Josef Dietrich, the highest-ranking defendant, stands to receive his number—11.

9–8. Romanian-born *Volksdeutscher* ex-Sturmmann Georg Fleps receives number 14 from the court.

9–9. First Lieutenant Lary declares, "This is the man (Fleps) that fired the first two pistol shots into the American prisoner of war."

9–10. Ex-Sturmmann Hans-Erick Lichtwarck of 2./SS-Panzer-Regiment 1 testifies for the prosecution and submits to cross-examination by Dr. Hans Hertkorn (*standing*) of the defense counsel on 21 May. To the left of Hertkorn is Hans Siptrott (number 60), Georg Fleps's tank commander. Immediately behind the woman seated at the left end of the defense counsel's table is Joachim Peiper, wearing a pair of sunglasses.

Following Lary's testimony, ex-Sturmmann Hans-Erick Lichtwarck of 2./SS-Panzer-Regiment 1 testified that his company commander, Hauptsturmführer Friedrich Christ, gave orders prior to the offensive that "no prisoners were to be taken in this combat." After receiving these orders, Lichtwarck joined his comrades of the 2. Kompanie in singing a popular song, "Sharpen the Long Knives!"

Sharpen the long knives! Sharpen the long knives!
    At the lamppost, blood should flow.
    The cudgels should fall quickly.
We don't care for the freedom of the Soviet Republic.

Asked whether the song in any way incited the German troops, Lichtwarck replied, "I don't think so." (9–10)

1st Lt. William R. Perl, an investigator of the Stavelot war crimes as well as of the Malmédy massacre, placed in evidence the various signed statements of the defendants (9–11). Much of his testimony and exhibits centered on the alleged orders passed down by the company commanders of *Kampfgruppe* Peiper. For example, ex-Obersturmführer Erich Rumpf, commander of the 9. Pionier-Kompanie of SS-Panzer-Regiment 1, stated that,

in early December, it was already clear that "the rules of warfare which, up to then, had been followed in the West, would not be strictly adhered to."

By Rumpf's account, the alleged regimental order read as follows:

All missions such as guarding prisoners of war and mopping up of villages belong to infantry accompanying the armored group, or directly following it. Therefore the situation may arise when prisoners of war have to be shot, and if necessary, the resistance has to be broken by terror.

The order also mentioned the Allies' bombing of German cities and the opportunity for revenge that the offensive might afford.

In another statement that Perl submitted, ex-Hauptscharführer Paul Ochmann admitted to shooting American POWs near Engelsdorf. He said he shot them in the back of the neck in accordance with the practice of the *Totenkopf Einheit* of which he had been a member earlier in the war.

Ochmann later alleged that his statement had been extracted under duress. The defense then asked Perl repeated

9–11. On 27 May, 1st Lt. William R. Perl—war crimes and Malmédy investigator, who interrogated many of the accused—answers questions posed by Lieutenant Colonel Ellis (*left*), trial judge advocate. A translator sits at center.

questions regarding his supposed mental and physical abuse of Ochmann, allegedly ranging from physical beatings to withholding food and asking Ochmann for his "last requests." Perl denied all allegations.

On 27 May, Kurt Framm, an ex-Untersturmführer who had been an adjutant on Pötschke's staff, testified for the prosecution. Many of the defendants heralded him with a chorus of raspberries (9–12). He testified that, prior to the Ardennes Offensive, Pötschke had told his subordinates that "this humanity business has stopped." Framm added that Peiper concurred, saying that the fighting would follow along the same lines as in Russia.

9–12. Kurt Framm, ex-Untersturmführer and adjutant on Werner Pötschke's staff, offers testimony on 27 May on behalf of the prosecution.

9–13. Ex-Pfc. Samuel Dobyns, former ambulance driver for the 575th Ambulance Company, 99th Infantry Division, points out the crossroads at Baugnez where he witnessed the massacre of members of the 285th Field Artillery Observation Battalion.

An important day in the trial came on 5 June when several key survivor witnesses, including Samuel Dobyns (9–13), Kenneth Ahrens, and Homer Ford, took the stand for the prosecution. For the benefit of the court's entourage, a large map board displayed the area surrounding Malmédy and Baugnez and *Kampfgruppe* Peiper's route.

Dobyns added a touch of humanity to the trial. Originally from the 99th Infantry Division, Dobyns said he had been swept up as a prisoner earlier in the day. At Baugnez,

an SS infantryman's conscience had moved him to save Dobyns from summary execution. Now, Dobyns searched the defendants' faces in an attempt to recognize this man (9–14). Ex-Sgt. Kenneth Ahrens (9–15 and 9–16) and ex-MP Homer D. Ford (9–17) likewise told their eyewitness stories.

The weight of the prosecution's evidence was so devastating in its sheer volume, not to mention in its emotional impact, that the defense had no choice but to begin

9–14. At the behest of the defense, Dobyns scans the seventy-four defendants to find the man who saved him from being shot at Baugnez. Defendant number 1 and the trial's official namesake, Valentin Bersin, sits on the first row of defendants.

9–15. Capt. Rafael Schumacker of the prosecution team shows ex-Sgt. Kenneth Ahrens an overlay map of the massacre site.

9–16. Ahrens demonstrates how he surrendered to elements of *Kampfgruppe* Peiper.

9–17. Homer D. Ford, an ex-MP who was on duty at Baugnez at the time of the massacre, relates his story to the court.

9–18. Called to testify for the defense, Gerhardt Engel—former commanding general of the 12. Volksgrenadier-Division during the Ardennes Offensive—testifies on 19 June. Note that while the SS prisoners were not permitted to wear any insignia, Engel's tunic still retains its red general officer collar tabs and epaulets.

chipping away at the multitude of assertions the prosecution laid down.

A most interesting witness appeared for the defense on 19 June—Gerhardt Engel, the commanding general of the 12. Volksgrenadier-Division during the Ardennes Offensive (9–18). Engel was one of the rebuttal witnesses called to dispute details of Josef Dietrich's sworn statement. Dietrich had claimed that Hitler had exhorted his commanders to "act with brutality" and "with no inhibitions" and that he said "a wave of terror and fright must precede us."

Professional soldier that he was, Engel appeared collected and cool before the court and gave discerning answers. His varied career had provided him with ample opportunity to observe Hitler in action, having served as army liaison officer in the *Führerhauptquartier* from 1938 to 1942. Engel's testimony concerned the content of a 12 December meeting with Hitler at Bad Nauheim. There, discussing the upcoming offensive, were Model, Keitel, Jodl, Rundstedt, Krüger, and the leaders of the I. SS-Panzerkorps.

According to Engel, when the offensive was discussed, Hitler laid out the war situation and called for the campaign to be pursued in a harsh and reckless manner, with the troops "rendered fanatical." Hitler did not specifically mention the treatment of prisoners, however, and certainly made no reference to increased brutality or a lack of inhibitions. Engel insisted that he definitely would have noticed anything in Hitler's instructions that would have changed the method of waging war.

Later on 19 June, Hermann Priess also testified about the Bad Nauheim meeting with Hitler. He corroborated Engel's testimony that the treatment of prisoners was not discussed. Furthermore, he recollected that, on 15 December, Dietrich personally delivered the tactical orders for 6. Panzer-Armee. These orders made *provisions for* (authors' italics) collection and transfer of prisoners. Priess noted that his corps did indeed take twenty-three hundred prisoners.

Just as Ochmann had, Priess complained of being mistreated during his interrogation. He said he had been confined in a dark cell and bombarded with dishonest (*sic*) questioning (9–19).

Joachim Peiper's testimony (9–20)—a large portion of which was a discourse on the operations of his *Kampfgruppe*—began on 21 June and extended over five days. He maintained that he had been incarcerated at Ruffenhausen in a darkened cell so small he could not move. During his time there he alleged that he was also hooded and beaten.

According to Peiper, Perl obtained Peiper's signed statement after confronting him with numerous state-

9-19. An emaciated Hermann Priess, former
commander of the I. SS-Panzerkorps, takes
the stand and undergoes cross-examination
by Morris Elowitz, the U.S. civilian assistant
trial judge advocate.

ments already signed by his comrades. Peiper's last "column of belief" in the comradeship "formed in blood at the front lines" crumbled as he read them. Despondent and believing that by taking full responsibility he would protect and free others, Peiper told Perl he would sign whatever was set in front of him.

Peiper emphatically denied that any regimental orders were issued on the days alleged by Hauptsturmführer Rumpf (possibly in an attempt to transfer guilt to his superiors). According to Peiper, no one at the regimental or company level knew of the coming offensive at that time. More important, Peiper likewise insisted that he saw no shooting of prisoners at Baugnez and that he only learned of the incident later at Ligneuville.

As the proceedings moved toward the close, one man—Marcel Boltz, an Alsatian who was assigned number 3 in photo 9–8—had all charges against him dropped. He was then handed over to the French for trial.

9-20. The star of the Malmédy trial,
ex-Obersturmbannführer Joachim
Peiper takes his seat on the
witness stand on 21 June.

9–21. Defendants on the officers' end of the dock listen to Dr. Otto Leiling (German defense counsel) translate Colonel Everett's concluding appeal for the defense. Front row, left to right: Dietrich (hidden by Leiling), Krämer, Priess, Peiper, and Friedrich Christ (number 7). Other *Kampfgruppe* company commanders are (second row immediately above Peiper) Vernoni Junker (number 29), commander of 6./SS-Panzer-Regiment 1, (third row) Erich Rumpf (number 54), commander of 9. Pionier-Kompanie, and (top row, directly above Krämer) Heinz Tomhardt (number 67), commander of 11./SS-Panzer-Regiment 1.

Dr. Otto Leiling of the German Defense Counsel translated for the defendants as Colonel Everett eloquently closed his arguments for the defense (9–21) with the following appeal: "He that would make his own liberty secure must guard even his enemy from oppression, for if he violates this duty, he establishes a precedent which will reach himself." For many of the seventy-three men whose lives were literally hanging in the balance, Everett's words were quite moving. Krämer wept openly. Priess and Peiper, however, appeared to listen sullenly, contemptuous of the proceedings. The court then recessed.

The wives of Josef Dietrich and Joachim Peiper entered the courtroom (9–22) after the recess. The court ignored Everett's appeal. On 11 July, it found all defendants guilty of the charges after only two hours and twenty minutes of deliberation.

Sentencing took place on 16 July (9–23). Judges warned the gallery to remain quiet during the reading of the sentences (9–24).

9–22. Following a recess on 11 June wives of defendants Dietrich and Peiper return to the courtroom to hear the court's verdict.

9-23. Dietrich and Krämer sit prepared to take notes during the final court session prior to sentencing on 16 July. Contemplating his fate on the third row, Gustav Knittel stares at Signal Corps photographer Pfc. Harry Bergmann. Note that Dietrich and Krämer have almost no shoelaces, most likely an antisuicide measure.

9-24. Spectators at the court in Dachau await the sentencing that would conclude the trial.

9–25. While Colonel Everett looks on at right, Priess receives a sentence of twenty years.

As a troubled Willis Everett looked on, one by one the defendants were called in alphabetical order up to the bench to receive their sentence (9–25, 9–26, and 9–27). Forty-three, including Peiper, received the death sentence; twenty-two, life imprisonment; and the remainder, ten to twenty years in prison.

However richly many of the defendants may have deserved their sentences, this trial was far from the finest hour of American justice. Even while the trial was under way, the prosecution admitted it had obtained confessions through the use of false witnesses, mock trials, and hoods—the latter signifying that the man's conviction was a forgone conclusion. In any honorable civilian court, this admission would have justified the judge in declaring a mistrial, but the Malmédy court apparently ignored it. Whether the misconduct was limited to falsehoods and harassment, as admitted, or included actual physical abuse, as some defendants claimed and as later alleged in the United States, it was still inexcusable.

All of this troubled Colonel Everett deeply. Saddled with the unenviable job of defending an assortment of highly unpopular clients, he could have simply gone through the motions without conviction or interest. But Everett did his best, and after the trial was over and he had returned to civilian life, he campaigned hard on behalf of his former clients. Eventually he reached the ear of Secre-

tary of the Army Kenneth Royal, who appointed the first of several review boards.

Then in March 1949 the Senate Armed Services Committee decided to investigate the trial and appointed a subcommittee to pursue the matter. This was a subject that deserved the best, most clearheaded of investigations, but unfortunately the subcommittee invited to participate a junior senator from Wisconsin named Joseph McCarthy. This was his first major opportunity to gain publicity and to make himself notorious, in both of which he succeeded thoroughly.

Eventually, however, all the death sentences were commuted to life imprisonment. Other sentences were reduced, and Peiper, the last of the prisoners in Landsberg, went free after serving eleven years. He was killed in 1976, however, when an inflammatory article in the French press incited someone to firebomb his home in Alsace.

MEMORIALS AND CEMETERIES

On 2 April 1950 a Signal Corps photographer took a photo of Bastogne to show how five years of peace had obliterated much of the war's scars (9–28). But the citizens' memories were still vivid.

9-26. Oswald Siegmund (number 58) leaves the courtroom at Dachau after being sentenced to death by hanging.

9-27. The last three defendants—(*left to right*) Paul Zwigart, Otto Wickmann, and Erich Werner—await their respective sentences of death, ten years, and life imprisonment.

9-28. Signal Corps photographer Genot visits Bastogne on 2 April 1950 and takes a photo (undoubtedly with a deliberate comparison in mind) from the same vantage point as photo 8-47. Five intervening years appear to have erased most of the war's damage.

9-29. In July 1950, the people of Belgium dedicated the Bastogne Memorial to the memory of all American troops killed in the Battle of the Bulge.

In July 1950, the Belgian people dedicated the Bastogne Memorial in honor of the Americans killed in the Battle of the Bulge (9–29). It is constructed in the shape of a star. The columns of the inner portion of the structure are inscribed with a history of the battle. Previously promoted to major general, McAuliffe was the main speaker at the dedication (9–30). He continued to attend the annual Bastogne Day ceremonies well into the postwar years (9–31).

At many different sites near Bastogne, and indeed throughout the Ardennes, various vehicles and other relics were preserved on the battlefields as monuments (9–32). Note that German shellfire struck this particular turret.

On 11 July 1960, the American Military Cemetery and Memorial at Ardennes, Belgium, was dedicated under the auspices of the American Battle Monuments Commission (9–33, 9–34, and 9–35). However sad it may be to reflect upon so many young men killed and later buried so far from home, no doubt most of them would be well content to rest with the comrades with whom they had fought and conquered.

9-30. Maj. Gen. Anthony McAuliffe delivers a speech to the people of Bastogne, July 1950.

9-31. McAuliffe places a wreath of flowers commemorating "Bastogne Day" in 1955.

9-32. On 14 June 1954, Belgian Lt. Henri LaFaut examines the turret of a Sherman tank mounted on a pedestal near Bastogne.

9-33. The American Military Cemetery and Memorial at Ardennes, Belgium, dedicated on 11 July 1960.

9–34. The American eagle watches over the fallen.

9–35. American defenders of Belgium at peace.

Appendix

COMPARATIVE RANK TABLE[*]

U.S Army Equivalent	German Army/Air Force	*Waffen-SS*
General of the Army	Generalfeldmarschall	Reichsführer-SS
General	Generaloberst	SS-Oberstgruppenführer
Lieutenant General	General der Artillerie	SS-Obergruppenführer
	der Infanterie	
	der Kavallerie	
	der Panzertruppen, etc.	
Major General	Generalleutnant	SS-Gruppenführer
Brigadier General	Generalmajor	SS-Brigadeführer
none	*none*	SS-Oberführer
Colonel	Oberst	SS-Standartenführer
Lieutenant Colonel	Oberstleutnant	SS-Obersturmbannführer
Major	Major	SS-Sturmbannführer
Captain	Hauptmann	SS-Hauptsturmführer
1st Lieutenant	Oberleutnant	SS-Obersturmführer
2d Lieutenant	Leutnant	SS-Untersturmführer
Sergeant Major	Stabsfeldwebel	SS-Sturmscharführer
Master Sergeant	Oberfeldwebel	SS-Hauptscharführer
Technical Sergeant	Feldwebel	SS-Oberscharführer
Staff Sergeant	Unterfeldwebel	SS-Scharführer
Sergeant	Unteroffizier	SS-Unterscharführer
Corporal	Obergefreiter	SS-Rottenführer
none	Gefreiter	SS-Sturmmann
Private, 1st Class	Oberschütze	SS-Oberschütze
Private	Schütze	SS-Schütze, SS-Mann

---

* There is disagreement among sources, particularly regarding corresponding American general officer ranks. For example, there were many more German *Generalfeldmarschalle* than American five-star generals.

Credits

All photographs, unless otherwise noted below, are courtesy of the National Archives of the United States.

Army War College: 2–16

Author's Collection: 1–25

Bundesarchiv: 1–18, 1–21, 1–22, 1–26, 1–27, 1–28, 1–29, 1–30, 1–32, 2–21, 3–3, 3–4, 3–5, 3–6, 3–7, 3–8, 3–10, 3–11, 3–12, 3–13, 3–14, 3–15, 3–17, 3–18, 3–19, 3–20, 3–22, 3–23, 3–24, 3–25, 3–26, 3–27, 3–28, 4–2, 4–3, 4–4, 4–5, 4–7, 4–8, 4–9, 4–10, 5–11, 5–22, 6–7, 6–18, 7–32, 7–33

National Air and Space Museum: 1–8, 1–11, 1–12, 1–14, 6–11, 7–2, 7–3, 7–4, 7–5, 7–6, 7–7, 7–8, 8–31

Maxwell Air Force Base: 1–10, 1–13, 2–68, 2–69, 2–70

James Weingartner Collection: 4–6

Index

U.S. FORCES AND EQUIPMENT

GERMAN FORCES AND EQUIPMENT

About the Authors

LT. COL. DONALD M. GOLDSTEIN, USAF (Ret.), is professor of public and international affairs at the University of Pittsburgh. CWO KATHERINE V. DILLON, USAF (Ret.), has collaborated with Dr. Goldstein on eleven books. J. MICHAEL WENGER is a military historian and writer residing in Raleigh, North Carolina. He has written for journals, newspapers, and the U.S. Marine Corps.